S0-BUF-789

# CHARLES LEONHARD
# American Music Educator

### by
### GEORGE N. HELLER

ML
423
.L29
H4
1995
West

**The Scarecrow Press, Inc.**
**Metuchen, N.J., & London**
**1995**

British Library Cataloguing-in-Publication data available

**Library of Congress Cataloging-in-Publication Data**

Heller, George N.
    Charles Leonhard:  American music educator / by
        George N. Heller.
    p.    cm.
    Includes bibliographical references and index
    ISBN 0-8108-2942-8
    1. Leonhard, Charles, 1915–    . 2. Music
        teachers—Illinois—Biography. I. Title.
ML423.L29H4  1995
780'.92—dc20
[B]                                                    94-30742

© George N. Heller, 1995
Manufactured in the United States of America
Printed on acid-free paper

# CONTENTS

# LIST OF ILLUSTRATIONS

# PROLOGUE

Charles Leonhard (b. 1915) is a member of the so-called G. I. Generation. His cohorts (born between 1901 and 1924) include U. S. presidents Kennedy, Johnson, Nixon, Ford, Carter, Reagan, and Bush. In other fields, this generation includes such luminaries as John Steinbeck, Walt Disney, Enrico Fermi, Marlene Dietrich, C. P. Snow, Simone de Beauvoir, Albert Camus, Tennessee Williams, Saul Bellow, Arthur Miller, Billy Graham, and Sir Edmund Hillary. Many male members of the G. I. Generation were among America's first Boy Scouts. The New Deal provided them with their first jobs. Some of them were old enough to fight in World War I. They were between the ages of five and twenty-eight in October of 1929, when the Great Depression began. All of them were old enough (and young enough) to fight in World War II.[1]

In music and music education, the G. I. Generation included Jascha Heifetz, Nelson Eddy, Louis Armstrong, William D. Revelli, Marian Anderson, Meredith Willson, Richard Rodgers, Bix Beiderbecke, Marguerite V. Hood, Roy Acuff, Vladimir Horowitz, Jimmy Dorsey, Glenn Miller, Bing Crosby, Count Basie, Louis G. Wersen, Gene Autry, Ethel Merman, Leroy Anderson, Gene Krupa, Benny Goodman, Samuel Barber, Robert A. Choate, Mahalia

[1]Neil Howe and William Strauss, *Generations: The History of America's Future, 1584–2069* (New York: William Morrow and Company, Inc., 1991), 161–278.

*Prologue*

Jackson, Stan Kenton, Woody Guthrie, John Cage, Perry Como, Allen P. Britton, Muddy Waters, Les Paul, Frank Sinatra, Robert Shaw, Ella Fitzgerald, Leonard Bernstein, Nat "King" Cole, Pete Seeger, Isaac Stern, Judy Garland, Hank Williams, and Henry Mancini.[2]

Charles Leonhard has been an important figure in the field of music education for over forty years. He spent most of that time at the University of Illinois as professor of music and chairman of graduate studies in music education. Leonhard's teaching and writing have been important to the field of music education. He influenced hundreds of students, and he introduced many new and significant ideas.

In his thirty-five years of teaching at the University of Illinois, as initiator and director of the doctoral program in music education, and in the years since his retirement, Professor Leonhard has been directly responsible for the education of numerous leaders in the field. Among these were such luminaries as Richard J. Colwell, founding editor of the *Bulletin of the Council for Research in Music Education* and recognized authority on music education evaluation and assessment; Bennett Reimer, John Beattie Professor of Music and Chairman of the Music Education Department at Northwestern University and author of *A Philosophy of Music Education*; and Eunice Boardman, formerly Director of the School of Music at the University of Wisconsin at Madison, now on the faculty at the University of Illinois, elementary music series author, and leader in music teacher education.

[2]George N. Heller, *Music and Music Education History: A Chronology* (Lawrence, KS: Department of Art and Music Education and Music Therapy, 1993), 32–50.

Professor Leonhard is probably identified to a greater extent than anyone else living or dead with the concept of music as aesthetic education. Prior to 1950, music was in the school curriculum primarily because of its instrumental values, its ability to enhance other, nonmusical qualities in students. Since 1950 and up to the present, thanks largely to the ideas of Leonhard and his students, the goals of music programs in schools have shifted toward developing students' aesthetic sensitivities. Methods and materials written and produced since about 1960 have increasingly reflected Leonhard's ideas along these lines.

Biography is one of the most important aspects of history. Ralph Waldo Emerson went so far as to say "There is no history, only biography."[3] The life and works of Charles Leonhard have had an enormous influence on music educators and music education in the second half of the twentieth century, and the story of his contributions is essential to an understanding of the development of music education as a profession.

To understand the course of music education in America for the past four decades, one can hardly overlook the work of Professor Leonhard and his students at the University of Illinois. Furthermore, students of this period may see his work as an extension of the Teachers College program in music education, particularly as the contributions of Peter W. Dykema (1873–1951) and James L. Mursell (1893–1963) shaped it. Leonhard studied with both of these giants, and he took many of his ideas and much of his inspiration from them.

[3]Ralph Waldo Emerson, "History," in *The Portable Emerson*, New Edition, ed. Carl Bode and Malcolm Cowley (New York: Viking Penguin, Inc., 1981), 119.

He established himself in the field just prior to the "Sputnik Era" and was most influential during the decades that followed. The story of his life and works offers a unique opportunity to study the tradition in music education whereby one generation hands down ideas and ideals to the next. Leonhard gave scores of students from Illinois what he had inherited from Dykema and Mursell and others at Teachers College, as well as the benefit of his own experience and intellect. His students, in turn, represent the legacy from Leonhard to the present which they will have passed to their students and which will continue well beyond the foreseeable future.

Doctoral students at the University of Illinois have undertaken some important studies of Leonhard's life and work. The first of these is Joe N. Prince's 1968 doctoral dissertation, written under Leonhard's supervision, which provides much useful information on the growth and development of the doctoral program at Illinois in the early years of Leonhard's tenure. Prince used primary sources to document the program, its relationship to the rest of the university, and the lives and works of key individuals.[4]

Albert D. Harrison's 1985 dissertation on the history of the School of Music at Illinois from 1940 to 1970 helps place Leonhard in his working environment during the first half of his career at Illinois. It also helps to explain some of the working relationships Leonhard had while on the faculty of the School of Music. Harrison's dissertation contains a few pages of biographical information on Leonhard, taken

[4]Joe N. Prince, "An Evaluation of Graduate Music Education Programs at the University of Illinois" (Ed.D. diss., University of Illinois, 1968).

from information Leonhard provided to him and not corroborated by independent sources.[5]

Judith A. Kritzmire studied Professor Leonhard's teaching, with particular emphasis on his class, Music 402 Analysis in Relation to Performance and Interpretation. She interviewed him on three occasions in 1986, and her dissertation contains considerable biographical information. While her primary source was Leonhard himself, she apparently did little checking or corroborating of what he told her. Kritzmire's study is a valuable one, though in need of verification and substantiation on many points. Nevertheless, it is helpful to check Harrison against Kritzmire for congruence, realizing, of course, that Kritzmire had access to Harrison's work for her study.[6]

Barbara L. Bennett has done extensive interviews of Leonhard during the period 1985–1990. She has also put together the Charles Leonhard Special Collection in Music Education at the School of Music, Baylor University, in Waco, Texas. The Collection contains materials, correspondence, manuscripts, and memorabilia. It also contains audio tapes, video tapes, and transcriptions of thirty-two interviews Bennett did with Leonhard pertaining to his personal life and professional activities. She has written two articles, one on Leonhard's work at the University of Illinois

[5]Albert D. Harrison, "A History of the University of Illinois School of Music, 1940–1970" (Ed.D. diss., University of Illinois, 1986).

[6]Judith A. Kritzmire, "The Pedagogy of Charles Leonhard: A Documentary Case Study" (Ed.D. diss. The University of Illinois, 1987).

making use of materials from the collection, and the other on the collection itself.[7]

This study presents three challenges. The first is to tell the story as completely as possible and to tell it in an interesting way. The second is to make sure that an accurate and balanced picture of the truth emerges in the story. The third is to establish the significance of Leonhard's life and works in the context of the times.

The first task is the easiest of the three. Leonhard has been very forthcoming in talking for the record and in providing copies of important documents. Furthermore, much of his work is a matter of public record. In recent years, Leonhard has spoken often and in depth on both his personal and his professional life. He has submitted documents to public scrutiny as no music educator has ever done, and he has made himself available almost without reservation for interviews by interviewers and oral historians. The man from Illinois has been especially prolific throughout his career, and his thoughts are thus quite accessible to the interested scholar. From his first publication in 1949 to his latest—which will no doubt come out long after this biography is published—Leonhard has made his thoughts and ideas about music education perfectly clear. They comprise an important part of the professional literature.

[7]Barbara L. Bennett, "The Leonhard Connection," *Bulletin of the Council for Research in Music Education* 110 (Fall 1991): 3–20; and Barbara L. Bennett, "The Charles Leonhard Oral History Memoirs," *Southeastern Journal of Music Education* 4 (1992): 84–100. See also Barbara L. Bennett, "Guide to the Charles Leonhard Special Collection in Music Education," TMs [photocopy], Charles Leonhard Special Collection in Music Education, School of Music, Baylor University, Waco, TX.

Getting an accurate and balanced picture of Leonhard's life and works is a bit more difficult than getting a detailed and interesting story. Leonhard is a strong personality who affects people in differing ways. To those who seek forceful leadership, he has something of a messianic quality. To those who prefer their leaders to be quiet and scholarly, he comes across as overly assertive, even aggressive. To those who seek diplomacy and subtlety in human relations, he appears somewhat boorish and blunt. With so much data coming directly from Leonhard himself, it is necessary to take into account the possibility of bias. To what extent has he unduly influenced the story? What has he not told? What has he glossed over? These are questions that must be answered in order to present a fair and honest portrait of the man and his times.

Significance, especially of recent historical figures, is always a tricky matter. Significance in the context of the times depends to a large extent on what else was going on. What may be a headline story in one era is relegated to lesser status in another. What seems terribly important at the time may, on reflection, turn out to be idiosyncratic or a passing fad. This is complicated in Leonhard's case by the fact that he tended to be something of a loner. He preferred to set trends rather than to follow them. He relied often on the force of his personality and the congeniality of circumstances to go his own way, and he has often spoken publicly against prevailing trends and the policies and procedures of some organizations.

Even about the matter of writing biography, Leonhard has spoken with his usual distinctive voice. In a session of the Music Educators National Conference in Chicago in

1984, Leonhard spoke in favor of biographical studies which "present a picture of the person as he really was—as a flesh and blood individual with foibles, prejudices, weaknesses, antagonisms, faults, and failures as well as virtues and achievements."[8]  While it is true that a subject with no faults and failures does not exist on the planet, it is also true that a person worthy of writing about is one whose merits far outweigh his or her negative qualities. Nevertheless, this biography follows Professor Leonhard's wishes to some extent in presenting him warts and all.

I am especially indebted to Professor Leonhard for his candor and willingness to lay his life open for scrutiny in this project.  Others who have contributed to the success of this effort have been librarians, especially all those at the Interlibrary Loan Services of The University of Kansas Libraries, whom I have visited almost weekly for most of the past five years, and to their counterparts at the University of Illinois who have supplied scores of books and dissertations.  I am grateful to  Bruce D. Wilson, Curator of the Music Educators National Conference Archives, Special Collections in Music, the University of Maryland, College Park, Maryland, for his collaboration in historical research for many years and for his contributions to this project.

I am also indebted to The University of Kansas for providing a sabbatical leave, during which I did much of the research, and to George L. Duerksen, Chair of the Music Education and Music Therapy Division,  for his support  and

---

[8]Charles Leonhard, "Where's the Beef?"  *The Bulletin of Historical Research in Music Education* 5 (July 1984):  59.

encouragement of music education research in general and this project in particular.

George N. Heller

The University of Kansas
Lawrence, Kansas
December 31, 1993

# CHAPTER I

# GROWING UP IN OKLAHOMA

Charles Leonhard was of European-American heritage. His parents were of solid Anglo-Saxon stock, and his childhood and youth bore marks of both Midwestern and Southern upbringing. His father was a stoic German-American, his mother an ebullient Scottish-American. Oklahoma in the early twentieth century was full of adventurers and opportunists of the sort often found on the frontier. The state was also home to Native Americans, many of whom were refugees from their homelands to the north and east, and to African-Americans, many of whom had come to the territory under duress. It was in this milieu, from 1915 to 1937, that Leonhard entered the world and learned how to function in it.

The Leonhard family was of German extraction. The ancestors of Charles's father, Morris Leonhard, came to the United States in 1870 to avoid conscription in the Kaiser's army. Morris was born in Meredosia, in west central Illinois, in 1874. His parents were wheat farmers in this small community on the Illinois River midway between the state capital and the Mississippi River. They became disenchanted with their life as middle American farmers and headed West. For a few years the Leonhards tried to make a living in California. Failing to find their fortune in the land of the gold rush, they returned to the Midwest, settling in

1

## Figure 1

### Oklahoma Before and After Statehood in 1907*

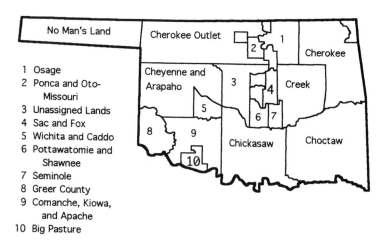

1 Osage
2 Ponca and Oto-
   Missouri
3 Unassigned Lands
4 Sac and Fox
5 Wichita and Caddo
6 Pottawatomie and
   Shawnee
7 Seminole
8 Greer County
9 Comanche, Kiowa,
   and Apache
10 Big Pasture

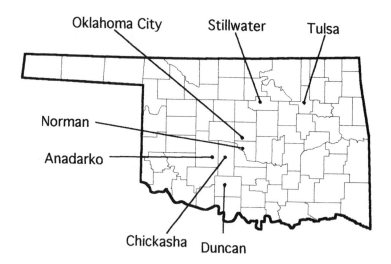

*From *Oklahoma: A History of Five Centuries*, by Arrell Morgan Gibson. Copyright © 1981 by the University of Oklahom Press. Used by permission.

Lawrence, Kansas. There Morris completed his education with the eighth grade. In Lawrence, the family worked the Robinson farm—named for its original owner, Charles Robinson, first governor of the state of Kansas.[1]

In 1899, Morris, weary of trying to scratch a living out of the Kansas soil, moved to Chickasha in the Indian Territory (now the State of Oklahoma) to try his hand in the retail hardware business. He worked until 1901 in a store owned by a man named Gilkey. Chickasha was a frontier town, founded in 1892 as a stop along the Rock Island railroad. By 1902 it had a population of 6,370. With the coming of Oklahoma statehood in 1907, Chickasha became the capital of Grady County. The Oklahoma College for Women was founded there by action of the state legislature in 1908.[2]

Anadarko (named for a branch of the Wichita tribe) was opened to settlement in 1901 along with the surrounding lands of the Kiowa-Comanche and Wichita tribes. Morris Leonhard moved to Anadarko in 1901 to set up his own business. The town is located on the Washita River about eighteen miles west of Chickasha on the Rock Island Railroad. It was at first a tent city, but it soon grew in size and population and prospered. Morris and a partner by the name of Duncan set up a hardware store in a tent and soon thereafter erected a three-story building to house their business. Anadarko became the county seat of Caddo County in 1907.[3]

[1]Charles Leonhard, Champaign, IL, to George N. Heller, Lawrence, KS, 1 January 1989, original in possession of the author.

[2]*The WPA Guide to 1930s Oklahoma* (Lawrence, KS: University Press of Kansas, 1986), 266–67.

[3]Leonhard to Heller, 1 January 1989; and *The WPA Guide to 1930s Oklahoma*, 268–269.

Figure 2

Corner of Broadway and First Street, Anadarko, Oklahoma*

*The location of Leonhard's father's hardware store.  Photograph
taken in February, 1990.

Soon after moving to Anadarko, Mr. Leonhard married Dora McRae from Chickasha. The McRae family was of Celtic origin. Dora was born in Alexander City, Alabama, in 1875 to a Confederate veteran and lumberman. Her mother had been a schoolteacher. According to Leonhard, "The McRaes were Celts who had been run out of Scotland by the English."[4] Charles's grandfather left Alabama as a fugitive, having tangled with a Union officer during the occupation of Alexander City. He lived for a while in Arlington, Texas, and Ryan, Oklahoma.

Leonhard takes a certain pride in his mother's ancestors, claiming that he inherited the extroverted side of his personality from them. "They were a wild bunch, and the wild streak persists in me to this very day. We all have various manifestations of what I call the 'McRae madness'."[5] He may have inherited his musical talent from his mother's side of the family as well.

Charles was probably aware of the musical talents on his mother's side of his family from a very early age. His aunt May McRae was about fifteen years older than Charles and about fifteen years younger than his mother. As a young child, Leonhard had heard his aunt May sing and play the piano, mostly by ear. His uncle Bill McRae was also a musician. "He was a roué of the first water. But nevertheless, he was really talented musically. He sang very well."[6]

Morris Leonhard and his new wife, Dora, immediately set about building a home and raising a family in Anadarko. The first child, Ruth, was born in Anadarko in January, 1903. She studied piano as a youngster and was the first in the family to go into music education. She was a choral

[4]Leonhard to Heller, 1 January 1989.

[5]Ibid.

[6]Kritzmire, "The Pedagogy of Charles Leonhard," 49.

## Figure 3

## 603 East Broadway, Anadarko, Oklahoma*

*The Leonhard family home. Photograph taken in February, 1990.

director in Oklahoma schools for about thirty years. In her retirement, she gave piano lessons in Clinton, Oklahoma.[7]

The second child in the Leonhard family was also a girl, May, who was born in 1905. She also went into education, though not in music. She taught in a two-room country school ten miles south of Anadarko, called the Buena Vista School, and later in a number of Oklahoma towns, including Carnegie, Watonga, and Anadarko. It was May who supported Charles in his early college years. "She was the one who really made it possible for me to go to the University of Oklahoma. She 'paid the freight' until, I guess, the second year." May died on October 17, 1989.[8]

Charles's older brother, Morris, Jr., nicknamed "Bus," was born in 1910. Bus graduated from Anadarko High School in 1928. He had been very active in high school. He was on the track team and played tennis. Bus had the lead in the junior play and belonged to a kind of school pep club called the Rednecks. He was also very active in music. Charles's brother sang in the glee club for three years and served as its president in his senior year. He also played clarinet in the school orchestra. Bus left for Tulsa soon after graduating from high school. He took a job with the WPA soon after the depression hit and eventually became a power in Oklahoma politics. He was the director

---

[7]Leonhard to Heller, 1 January 1989; and Kritzmire, "The Pedagogy of Charles Leonhard," 39–50.

[8]Charles Leonhard, quoted in Kritzmire, "The Pedagogy of Charles Leonhard," 55; Charles Leonhard, Champaign, IL, to George N. Heller, Lawrence, KS, 23 January 1990, original in possession of the author; and Charles Leonhard, Urbana, IL, to George N. Heller, Lawrence, KS, 25 March 1993, original in possession of the author.

of the Oklahoma Employment Security Commission until
shortly before his death in 1975.[9]

The fourth and final Leonhard child, Charles, was
born on December 8, 1915.  Like his two sisters and his
brother, he first saw the light of day in the family home on
East Broadway near the main four corners of Anadarko. Dr.
Anderson, the family physician, delivered Charles, as he had
the other three Leonhard children.[10]

The Leonhard children's father and Mr. Duncan must
have done well in the turn-of-the-century booming Sooner
state.  In the tumultuous frontier life that was Oklahoma in
the pre–dust bowl days, these two young entrepreneurs soon
had branch stores in Hinton and three other nearby
communities.  New immigrants to the territory established
communities at a rapid pace, and Morris Leonhard was no
exception.  He prospered in retail sales and soon became a
pillar of Anadarko.  He served on the school board and was
a leader in the Methodist Church, as well as numerous other
groups.

The Leonhard and Duncan building at the corner of
Broadway and First Street in the heart of Anadarko had a
special attraction that must have influenced the children in the
impressionable years of their youth. It had an "opera house"
on the third floor.  This was a typical nineteenth-century
American establishment which was a combination
community theater, meeting house, and all-purpose social
center.  Melodramas, lectures, magic shows, concerts, and
other assorted wonders were typical fare in this facility on

---

[9]Marie Cummins (Mrs. Truman) Melton, interview by George N.
Heller, 12 February 1990, Anadarko, OK, tape recording and transcript in
possession of the author. Mrs. Melton was a classmate of Leonhard in the
Anadarko schools, and she had a 1928 *Caddo*, the Anadarko High School
yearbook, which contained much information on Morris Leonhard, Jr.
("Bus"). See also, Kritzmire, "The Pedagogy of Charles Leonhard," 44–45.

[10]Leonhard to Heller, 1 January 1989; and Kritzmire, "The Pedagogy
of Charles Leonhard," 39.

the top of Charles's father's store. Entertainers on the Redpath Circuit, appeared often. One of these whom Leonhard later recalled was the industrialist and financial nabob, Chauncey de Pugh, who came to Anadarko to deliver a lecture.[11] Perhaps this early contact with the stage and with entertaining audiences convinced the young Charles that he should pursue some kind of career in show business. As early as age five (in 1920) he discovered that "I could sing like a goddamned bird and could hold an audience in the palm of my hand singing. I sang frequently and when I sang 'When You and I were Young, Maggie,' there was not a dry eye in the house."[12] Two years later, he found a similar talent at the keyboard: "In 1922 [Leonhard made] the discovery that I could likewise hold an audience playing the piano."[13]

This idyllic childhood for Charles was short-lived, however. Morris began to get involved in the darker side of Oklahoma public affairs and political life, when, during World War I, he spent a good deal of his time working to get German-Americans out of jail. Oklahomans were incarcerating his fellow Teutons in the racial and ethnic hysteria that swept the state and the nation in the late teens and throughout the 1920s. A "Council for Defense" worked to have people arrested during the war simply for having a German surname or for speaking with an accent. This was the era of the Ku Klux Klan, which prospered in those intolerant times, and of the Scopes "Monkey Trial" (1925).[14]

[11]Kritzmire, "The Pedagogy of Charles Leonhard," 38.

[12]Leonhard to Heller, 1 January 1989.

[13]Ibid.

[14]Ibid.; see also Gibson, *Oklahoma: A History*, 214–220.

Things went quickly from bad to worse as the family was plunged with the rest of the state into the depths of the Depression. Financial upheaval came to the lower midwest much sooner than to the rest of the country. A severe post World War I recession that deepened into a depression as grain and beef prices declined affected Oklahoma. Banks began to foreclose and then fail, and workers went out on frequent strikes in efforts to improve their wages and living conditions.

As the economy of the state went bad, Morris lost his money and his stores in 1920. The family retained a farm Mrs. Leonhard had purchased with her "pin money" in better times. Morris and his children raised hogs for one year, but the animals all died in a hog cholera epidemic that swept through the country. After that he went into the dairy business and was somewhat successful.[15]

From about age ten on, Leonhard practiced the piano while his father milked the cows in the dairy. Father and son typically delivered milk after supper to houses all over town in a Model T Ford. "Thus my schedule was fairly rigorous: up at 5:00 a.m. to go to the farm to milk the cows by hand; walk to school at 8:00 a.m.; walk to and from home (1 mile each way) for lunch between 12:00 noon and 1 p.m.; leave school at 4:00 p.m.; practice from 4:30 to 6:30; eat supper; deliver milk 7:30 to 8:30 or 9:00 p.m.; do homework from 9:00–10:00 p.m. and to bed."[16]

Mrs. Leonhard helped the family by taking a job. Falling back on her early training, she took a job as a milliner at the Fair department store in Anadarko. Not one to begrudge her husband's political activism in behalf of social justice, she also became involved in the Delphian Club and the Women's Christian Temperance Union. Perhaps both

[15]Leonhard to Heller, 1 January 1989; and Leonhard to Heller, 25 March 1993; and Kritzmire, "The Pedagogy of Charles Leonhard," 40–42.

[16]Leonhard to Heller, 25 March, 1993. See also Melton interview.

Figure 4

Charles Leonhard in the Seventh Grade (1927-28)

*Photograph courtesy Marie Cummins (Mrs. Truman) Melton, Anadarko, OK.

these activities were related to the enactment of prohibition in 1919 and the passage of women's suffrage of 1920.[17]

Young Charles began to immerse himself in music. He took piano lessons from a local teacher, Mrs. Elizabeth Bettis Lawrence, whom Leonhard called "Mrs. Bess Lawrence," in 1925. Mrs. Lawrence was from Tennessee and had studied piano at Carson-Newman College in Jefferson City, Tennessee. She had also studied at Martha Washington College in Abington, Virginia, and the Virginia Institute in Bristol, Virginia. She had once taken private lessons with William H. Sherwood (1854–1911). Sherwood was a student of William Mason (1829–1908), son of the famous music educator, Lowell Mason.[18]

The budding musician's daily routine consisted of doing chores on the farm, going to school, and practicing two hours a day after school. He claims to have had no social life during this period, "but being an introvert and loving the piano, I really did not miss it."[19] Still, he must have felt the dramatic change in life style at some level. Following his father's financial difficulties, Leonhard and his family "were as poor as church mice and literally sold milk to buy bread, but followed the Southern style in keeping up appearances."[20]

---

[17]Kritzmire, "The Pedagogy of Charles Leonhard," 40–43.

[18]"Early History of Anadarko," loose leaf material on file in the Anadarko Philomathic Museum, Anadarko, OK, 57, 58. See also *The New Grove Dictionary of American Music*, 1986, s.v. "Sherwood, William H.," by Robert W. Groves. Mrs. Lawrence also taught music at the Carson-Newman College and at the Ohio Valley College in Sturgis, Kentucky. She had taught private piano lessons in Morristown, Tennessee, and Cisco, Texas, before coming to Anadarko in about 1910. She was supervisor of music in the Anadarko schools for two years and had many students in private piano and voice. Mrs. Lawrence was the choir director in the Baptist church in Anadarko, apparently with great success, for many years. She was married to Caddo County Judge Robert Lee Lawrence and had four children.

[19]Leonhard to Heller, 1 January 1989.

[20]Ibid.

At some point, Leonhard must have realized that his musical ability was an entrée to other worlds and broader experiences. His piano teacher began his education in the ways of the wider world with many an adventure. "Having learned to drive at the age of ten, I drove Mrs. Lawrence, my piano teacher, to Oklahoma City in her Apperson Jackrabbit which was the largest car I have ever seen."[21] Many great pianists toured the country, and Oklahoma had its fair share of visiting artists of world renown. In his youth, Leonhard heard many of them, including Ignace Jan Paderewski, Josef Hofmann, Harold Bauer (with whom he later studied), Sergey Rachmaninoff, Artur Schnabel, and Josef Lhévinne.[22]

His classmates thought him to be a very private person, gifted with musical talent and intelligence. One of Leonhard's classmates from Anadarko, Marie Cummins (Mrs. Truman) Melton, also known as Penny, said that "Charles just came to school and went home. Now if he had outside activities, hobbies, and things, I didn't know. Neither did anyone else . . . . But I know they just used him all the time. You know, because they'd say, 'Well, Charles will play for us.' They'd just understand, you see, they didn't have to go out and try to recruit someone to play some little old something. Because it was just his life, I guess."[23]

Penny Melton also thought that Charles did well in his school work, but that he did not share his academic gifts with classmates. "Well, now, he was smart. He was very smart. . . . But, yet, now he wasn't one of these kids who would let you copy off his paper, I'm sure, like the rest of us. It was horrible."[24]

[21]Leonhard to Heller, 1 January 1989.

[22]Leonhard to Heller, 23 March 1993.

[23]Melton interview.

[24]Ibid.

One gets a picture of Leonhard as a shy, serious student and budding musician in his Anadarko years. "Charles always wore his hair kind of long and kind of hung down. And, you know, kids, they'd say, 'Well you know, he's really a genius, you know, and he's really intelligent.' And then he'd get up there, and of course he could just make that piano talk, you know. But mostly what we liked then was old jivin' stuff, you know. And of course he'd sit down and play the classical. It was very beautiful."[25]

After five years of study with Mrs. Lawrence, the thirteen-year old student from Anadarko changed piano teachers to study with Lois Bennett. Miss Bennett was then professor of piano performance at the Oklahoma College for Women (now the University of Science and Arts) in Chickasha. She had studied at the New England Conservatory and was very knowledgeable about life beyond the Oklahoma borders. Miss Bennett had also studied piano in Europe.[26]

From 1928 until his graduation from high school in 1933, Leonhard drove to Chickasha for free weekly lessons with Miss Bennett. "In many respects she was the most potent influence on my development. She gave me comps [complimentary tickets] for all the concerts at the College including Myra Hess for whom I played and with whom I had tea at Miss Bennett's house after Hess's concert."[27]

Mrs. Lawrence and Miss Bennett had introduced Leonhard to the world of competition in music. They prepared him to play in county, district, and state piano contests. At the age of ten, in 1925, Leonhard won first

---

[25]Melton interview.

[26]*The Argus* (1929), 26; *The Argus* (1930), 27; and *The Argus* (1931), 26. These were the yearbooks for the Oklahoma College for Women. They are presently located in the University Archive, University of Science and the Arts, Chickasha, OK.

[27]Leonhard to Heller, 1 January 1989.

place in a county piano contest competing in the elementary division. He remembers not wanting to play the contest wearing short pants which were the style of the day for boys his age, refusing to play unless he could wear his overalls. After that, he dressed as the occasion demanded.[28]

In his sophomore year of high school, Leonhard participated in the state music contests, held that year in Stillwater at Oklahoma Agricultural and Mechanical College (now Oklahoma State University). At that time (the spring of 1931), the music contests in Oklahoma, as elsewhere, were judged on a ranking system (first, second, third place, and so forth) rather than a rating system (first, second, third division, and so forth). Charles took first place in Stillwater in 1931. This experience was to lead him into contact with future music teachers and other influences that would advance his career in music education.[29]

Leonhard's participation in piano contests was somewhat traumatic for him. He disliked the whole experience, but his mother insisted on his going. She was both a source of support and something of a pusher in this process. "We drove all over Oklahoma to Weatherford, Norman, Stillwater—wherever the contest took place. Inevitably the tension was such that I always had to stop the car on the way home and vomit. She was a determined woman and played something approaching the role of a 'stage mother'."[30]

From about 1925 until 1933, Leonhard and his mother travelled the State of Oklahoma in their Model T Ford, with the young boy at the wheel. At that time the State had few paved roads, and often the highway signs were rudimentary

[28]Leonhard to Heller, 25 March 1993.

[29]"Stillwater, Bristow Are High in Instrumental Work," *Daily O'Collegian* [the Oklahoma A & M student newspaper], 8 May 1931, 1; and Kritzmire, "The Pedagogy of Charles Leonhard," 54.

[30]Leonhard to Heller, 25 March 1993.

Figure 5

Anadarko High School*

*Currently a fifth grade attendance center. Photograph taken in February 1990.

at best. Leonhard recalls simply heading in the general direction of a town and following section line roads until he and his mother could figure out where they were and how to get where they wanted to go. Because the contests were in the spring, much of the travel was through miles of Oklahoma red mud.[31]

Leonhard's high school education is remarkable only in that it was much like countless others of his generation. He graduated in the spring of 1933 with three units of English, one of math, two and one-half of social studies, two of language, one and one-half of science, and one of music. His senior class consisted of twenty-six boys and forty-two girls. The attendance record for 1932–33 shows that Charles had been absent for six and one-half days in the first semester of his senior year and five and one-half days in the spring.[32]

His claim that he buried himself in household chores and practicing the piano in lieu of a normal social life appears to be valid. He seems to have remembered little of his school music life or of the popular music of his day. Such tunes as "Ain't Misbehavin'" and "Singin' in the Rain" (1929), "Embraceable You" and "I Got Rhythm" (1930), "Mood Indigo" and "When the Blue of the Night Meets the Gold of the Day" (1931), "Brother Can You Spare a Dime?" and "I'm Gettin' Sentimental Over You" (1932), and "The Last Round-Up" and "Smoke Gets in Your Eyes" (1933) don't hold much of a place in his recollections.

The University of Oklahoma accepted Leonhard as a student on September 18, 1933. This began his life-long adventure in higher education. He started out in a liberal arts

---

[31]Leonhard to Heller, 25 March 1993.

[32]Charles Leonhard, Transcript of Work at the University of Oklahoma, Issued to the Student, 14 September 1937, photocopy in possession of the author; and "Oklahoma Teacher's Register of Attendance and Scholarship, Grade 10 through 12, 1932–1936," Principal's Office, Anadarko High School, Anadarko, OK.

program, not in music education. During his first term in Norman, Leonhard studied beginning French, Latin (Cicero), United States Government, English Composition, and Military science. He belonged to a national honor freshman fraternity, Phi Eta Sigma, in 1933–1934.[33]

The University required all male students to enroll in military science for two years. This experience would serve Leonhard well, as it paid a stipend covering tuition in later years. It also gave him an advantage in choice of military occupational specialty when World War II came, but in 1933 he simply took it because it was required. In the spring semester of 1934, he took the same courses, except for a course in harmony which he took in place of United States Government.[34]

During his sophomore year, Leonhard enrolled in Educational Psychology, Botany, French Composition, History of Western Civilization, Military Science, and Piano. He also began a three-year stint as the accompanist for the University of Oklahoma Men's Glee Club. Working with R. Heber Richards, conductor of the glee club, was another experience that contributed to his wealth of knowledge about music and music education. Richards was a professor in public school music at the University of Oklahoma in 1933. He had earned a Bachelor of Music degree from Ohio Northern University in 1905 and had been on the Oklahoma faculty since 1924.[35]

In later years, Leonhard recollected with fond memories the years 1934–37, when he was "a pianist for the

[33]Leonhard to Heller, 1 January 1989; and *Sooner* (1934), 218. The *Sooner* was the University of Oklahoma Yearbook. Copies are located in the University Archive, Western History Collection, University of Oklahoma, Norman, OK.

[34]Leonhard to Heller, 1 January 1989; and Leonhard, University of Oklahoma Transcript.

[35]University of Oklahoma, *University of Oklahoma Catalog*, 1932–33 (Norman, OK: University of Oklahoma, 1932), 311.

OU men's Glee Club under the direction of R. H. Richards, a Welshman, who was choral director at OU. I learned most of what I know about choral conducting and choral rehearsing from working with Richards."[36]

Leonhard's piano teacher at the University was Lyman Stanley. Professor Stanley, like Lois Bennett, wa: graduate of the New England Conservatory. He had taught at Oklahoma from 1920 to 1923 and later from 1934 until sometime after 1942.[37] The young college student from Anadarko studied with Stanley and became something of a surrogate son. "He and his wife Blanche nurtured me in every way–musically, nutritionally with frequent dinners at their home and personally."[38]

The University charged special fees for lessons over and above the cost of tuition. To help pay these, Mr. Stanley arranged a job for Leonhard as manager of student recitals. The job paid a salary equal to the extra fees for his piano lessons. Leonhard carried a great respect and admiration for Mr. Stanley throughout his career. "He was a great man, a fine teacher, and a great friend, until he died in the 1970s."[39]

In the summers of 1933, 1934, and 1935, Leonhard gave piano lessons in and around his home town of Anadarko, including the towns of Apache, Gracemont, and Lookeba. "The summer of 1935, my father, being a good Democrat, got me a job measuring acreage on cotton farms to ensure that farmers did not exceed their acreage allotment

[36] Leonhard to Heller, 1 January 1989.

[37] Roy Gittinger, *The University of Oklahoma, 1892–1942* (Norman, OK: University of Oklahoma, 1942), 117; and University of Oklahoma, *University of Oklahoma Catalog*, 1936–37 (Norman, OK: University of Oklahoma, 1936).

[38] Leonhard to Heller, 1 January 1989.

[39] Leonhard to Heller, 1 January 1989. See also Kritzmire, "The Pedagogy of Charles Leonhard," 54.

assigned by the Agriculture department. Not having a car, I rode a horse all over Caddo County doing this job."[40]

The Great Depression placed many a hardship on college students from families of modest means in the 1930s. Leonhard met the challenge as did many of his peers by putting small amounts of money together from a variety of sources. His sister, May, helped out the first two years, and Lyman Stanley arranged for him to manage recitals. He also earned about ten dollars a month tutoring well-to-do undergraduate students in French, and he had help from the National Youth Administration, the Reserve Officers Training Corps (ROTC), and the Lew Wentz Foundation.[41]

In the spring semester of his sophomore year, Leonhard continued on his liberal arts course, with a little music thrown in. For the spring semester, 1935, he enrolled in Botany, Harmony, French Readings, Piano, French Composition, and Military Science. He continued to study piano with Mr. Stanley and to accompany Richards's men's glee club. He was also a member of the University of Oklahoma French Club.[42]

In the fall of 1935, Leonhard reached a major decision point in his life. His college transcript shows that he enrolled in Oklahoma History, French Pronunciation, Music Appreciation, Intermediate Algebra, Practical French, and Spanish Composition, but then withdrew from all these courses. He changed his major from French to music education and subsequently added Advanced Harmony,

[40]Leonhard to Heller, 25 March 1993.

[41]The National Youth Administration had been created by executive order of Franklin Delano Roosevelt on 26 June 1935. It provided funds for part-time employment of needy students between the ages of sixteen and twenty-four to help them remain in school. See Lawrence A. Cremin, *American Education: The Metropolitan Experience, 1876–1980* (New York: Harper & Row Publishers, Inc., 1988), 311. The Lew Wentz Foundation was the benefaction of an Oklahoma oil man. See Leonhard to Heller, 1 January 1989, and Kritzmire, "The Pedagogy of Charles Leonhard," 55–56.

[42]*Sooner* (1937), 74.

Piano, Voice, String Instrument Methods, Sight Singing, Violin Class, and Military Science. He did this on the advice of Professor Richards.[43]

In the spring of 1936, Leonhard continued with his music education program by taking Advanced Harmony, Piano, Teaching Music in High School, Voice, Music History, Sight Singing, Conducting Vocal Organizations, and Military Science. Possibly because he had fallen behind with his transfer of majors, that summer (1936), Leonhard took a course in educational psychology from the Southwest State Teachers College in Weatherford. He also spent the summer of 1936 in ROTC Camp, for which he received credit on his University of Oklahoma transcript.[44]

Leonhard packed his senior year at Oklahoma full of courses. In the fall term, he took Music Appreciation, Advanced Sight Singing, Military Science, Foundations of Education, Voice, Counterpoint, Piano, Curriculum in the Secondary School, Student Teaching in the Junior High School, and Music History. His transcript shows that he enrolled in, but withdrew from, Applied Aesthetics, Teaching Elementary School, and Orchestration. He passed his piano proficiency exam in the Spring of 1937 and took Student Teaching in the Junior High School, Advanced Sight Singing, Piano, Military Science, Orchestration, Double Counterpoint, Measurement for Secondary School, U. S. History, and Student Teaching in the Secondary School. He earned the Bachelor of Fine Arts degree in Public School Music on June 7, 1937.[45]

[43]Leonhard, University of Oklahoma Transcript; and Leonhard to Heller, 1 January 1989.

[44]Leonhard, University of Oklahoma Transcript; and Leonhard to Heller, 23 January 1990.

[45]Leonhard, University of Oklahoma Transcript; Leonhard to Heller, 23 January 1990; and Leonhard, Diploma for Bachelor of Fine Arts in Public School Music, University of Oklahoma, 1937, photocopy in possession of the author.

Leonhard gave solo recitals all three years he studied with Lyman Stanley. Among these were two concerts in which Leonhard played piano concertos. On these occasions, Stanley played the orchestral parts on the organ. Leonhard also was busy as a student accompanist while in school. He played for two voice recitals each of his last two years, both by Adrian Wynobel, who was on the faculty and was Leonhard's own voice teacher.[46]

Leonhard had not only completed the requirements for a Bachelor of Fine Arts degree in Public School Music, but was also within one course of a second bachelor's degree in piano. He tried to complete this by enrolling in a course in orchestration in the spring of 1938, but had to withdraw from the course. He managed to complete the course by correspondence in the Fall semester of 1938 and was awarded a Bachelor of Music degree in Piano on 5 June 1939.[47]

At the age of twenty-one Charles Leonhard went out into the world to seek a job as a music teacher. His youth was over. His parents had given him life, nurtured him, and instilled basic attitudes and values into his personality. His public school teachers, classmates, friends, and acquaintances in Anadarko had done likewise. It was time for him to assume his role in the adult world. For young Mr. Leonhard, this would start out gradually.

Like most people at this particular time, Charles Leonhard had very little idea of what was in store for him. He separated himself from home slowly and made his way into the world of work as an independent adult. He did this in almost total ignorance of the impending cataclysm that was to shake the nation so dramatically in December of 1941. So far as Leonhard was concerned, in the summer of

---

[46]Leonhard to Heller, 25 March 1993.

[47]Leonhard's University of Oklahoma transcript; and Leonhard to Heller, 23 January 1990.

1937, he would find a job, perhaps go to graduate school, and live out his life in Oklahoma, teaching music to high school students.

# CHAPTER II

# PUBLIC SCHOOL TEACHING CAREER

Charles Leonhard left the University of Oklahoma in Norman and headed sixty-five miles south and slightly west down the Rock Island Railway to his first teaching position in Duncan. Like Anadarko, Duncan had its first European-American settlers in 1901 after many years of being held in reserve as tribal land. By 1937, stock raising, farming and the oil industry had helped develop Duncan into a good-sized marketing center for the region. When Leonhard arrived in the fall of 1937, the town had about 7,500 residents. In 1941, the year he left Duncan, the school system had 2,500 students and 56 teachers. In Leonhard's day the schools were segregated. African-American students attended their own elementary school, and then they went to a separate high school, both of which were located in the southern part of the town.[1]

The high school for European-American students in Duncan was located on Ninth Street between Ash and Oak streets, just three blocks from the downtown business district. It was one year old in the summer of 1937, and the auditorium wing had just been completed. Just two blocks west of the school, at 1115 West Oak was Leonhard's residence while he taught in Duncan. It was in a private

---

[1]*The WPA Guide to 1930s Oklahoma*, p. 375.

Figure 6

Duncan High School, Duncan, Oklahoma*

*Now the Duncan Junior High School. This photograph taken in February, 1990.

home, owned by the Tucker family. The young man lived within easy walking distance of his job, downtown shopping, and church.

Leonhard's first position in the Duncan schools was as director of choral music at the high school. He succeeded a choral teacher who also taught English at the high school. The enrollment in choral music was low, and the administration wanted some improvement in both the quality of the program and in the number of students participating in it.[2]

His first teaching schedule in the fall of 1937 was music theory class first period, boys' glee club second period, and girls' glee club fifth period. In between second and fifth period at the high school, he went over to the junior high and taught some general music classes. Leonhard was one of two members of the music department at Duncan High. Raymond Culp had the instrumental program.[3]

Norval George was the Superintendent of Schools in Duncan, and it was he who hired Leonhard. Mr. George was working on a doctoral degree at Peabody College for Teachers in Nashville at the time, and he sometimes came up with ideas from his graduate studies that he tried out on the teachers in Duncan.[4]

The Duncan schools paid Leonhard a beginning teacher's salary of 100 dollars a month, which amounted to 900 dollars for the school year of 1937–38. In December, he reported to Mr. George, the Superintendent, that he had an offer to become a commander of a Civilian Conservation

[2]Charles Leonhard, interview by author, 13 October 1990, Urbana, IL, tape and transcript in possession of the author.

[3]"Subjects High School Faculty Will Teach This Year Listed," *The Duncan* [Oklahoma] *Banner*, 2 September 1937, 1; "Banquet for Teachers Has Big Attendance," *The Duncan Banner*, 21 November 1937, 7.

[4]Leonhard interview, 13 October, 1990.

Figure 7

Leonhard's Residence at 1115 Oak Street,
Duncan, Oklahoma*

*This is where Leonhard lived while teaching in Duncan. A family named Tucker owned the home. It is located two blocks west of the school. Photograph taken in February, 1990.

Corps Camp for 125 dollars a month. George immediately raised his salary to 125 dollars a month. Leonhard also gave twenty piano lessons a week which earned him another 100 to 125 dollars a month, thereby nearly doubling his income.[5]

Once the school year had gotten well under way, Leonhard gave a progress report to the school board. He told members of the board that most of the boys he had auditioned wanted to sing bass and baritone, but that few wanted to sing tenor. In colorful language of the sort he would favor throughout his career, Leonhard told a reporter for the local paper that "Tenors are scarcer at Duncan High School than traffic lights on Main Street." He added that "It seems that high school boys consider baritones and basses more manly than tenors, and they all want to sing deep, whether they can or not."[6]

In characteristic tone, Leonhard told the board: "Of course, that's nonsense." In case anyone did not get the point, Leonhard said that without a decent tenor, his boys quartet was just a deep trio and that his boys' glee club would sound "like somebody turned the tone control all the way over to the left."[7]

Early in the fall term, Leonhard gave the first of his many public performances in the community. On October 11, 1937, he gave a public recital on the piano at the Junior High School. Years later, his principal Dion C. Wood recalled that Leonhard was something of a showman at the keyboard, affecting mannerisms of the finest keyboard

[5]Charles Leonhard, Urbana, IL, to George N. Heller, Lawrence, KS, 17 May 1993, original in possession of the author.

[6]"Tenors Scarce at Duncan High; All Boys Want to Sing Bass," *The Duncan Banner*, 5 October 1937.

[7]Ibid.

performers of his day, adjusting the stool and tugging at his sleeves before beginning to play.[8]

All the while he was in Duncan, Leonhard kept up regular piano practice. He also gave private piano lessons after school and on Saturdays. On a Saturday afternoon in October of 1937, Leonhard was a special guest of the regular meeting of the Duncan Music Club. He played the Chopin Waltz in A-Flat for the formal program and an additional selection during the social hour.[9]

Leonhard joined in both sacred and secular choral activities in the community. He sang in the Methodist Church choir in Duncan. His colleague, Lauraleen Farnham Moore, was the organist, and a Mrs. Robins directed the choir. Mrs. Moore was also the choral music teacher at the Junior High School. She had been teaching part time and in various capacities several years before Leonhard's arrival. While he was there she taught required general music courses in the seventh and eighth grades.[10]

Leonhard also became assistant choral director for the Duncan Choir Guild in the fall of 1937. As a representative of that group, he was one of two delegates to the district

[8]"Leonhard to Give Recital," *The Duncan Banner*, 6 October 1937; and Dion C. Wood and LaVerne Moore Smith, interview by author, 11 February 1990, Duncan, OK, tape recording and transcript in possession of the author. Mr. Wood was principal at Duncan High School all the while Leonhard taught there; Mrs. Smith was a student at Duncan High School, class of 1941.

[9]Leonhard to Heller, 8 June 1989; see also, Kritzmire, "The Pedagogy of Charles Leonhard," 56; Leonhard to Heller, 1 January 1989; and "Two New Members Are Welcomed into Duncan Music Club," *The Duncan Banner*, 10 October 1937, 7.

[10]Leonhard to Heller, 1 January 1989; Leonhard interview, 13 October 1990; and Leonhard to Heller, 17 May 1993.

Figure 8

Charles Leonhard at the Keyboard*

*Demon Round-Up* [Duncan, Oklahoma, High School Yearbook] (1941), 43.

meeting of the National Federated Music Clubs held in Lawton, Oklahoma, on November 13, 1937.[11]

Leonhard's first public performance with school groups came in November, 1937 at the annual Education Week celebration given by the Junior-Senior High School Parent-Teachers Association. His boys' quartet sang two numbers, the girls' quartet sang "Flow Gently, Sweet Afton," and two students sang a duet, "Billy Boy." Leonhard accompanied each group on piano.[12]

At the Duncan Chamber of Commerce annual banquet for Stephens County school teachers, Leonhard's groups again provided music in November of 1937. The audience consisted of 162 teachers from the county's schools and over one-hundred Duncan businessmen. According to *The Duncan Banner*, Leonhard's boys' quartet sang several selections. One of these was a parody on the teachers. The students set a good-natured ribbing of Leonhard's colleagues to "a popular tune of other years."[13]

In December, Leonhard's junior high students presented an operetta, "The Moon Maiden." The cast included twelve major parts and a chorus of twenty boys and girls. The students gave two performances of the operetta during the school day for the elementary grades and for the junior and senior high schools and an evening performance for the community.[14]

[11]Lauraleen Farnham Moore (Mrs. Charles) Walker, interview by author, 10 February 1990, Duncan, OK, tape recording and transcript in possession of the author; "Choir Guild to Be Active in Second Year," *The Duncan Banner*, 19 October 1937, 8; and "Choir Guild Chooses Two," *The Duncan Banner*, 9 November 1937, 6.

[12]"School Parade Today Moved to Later Date," *The Duncan Banner*, 10 November 1937, 1.

[13]"Banquet for Teachers has Big Attendance."

[14]"Junior High's Operetta to Be Ready Friday," *The Duncan Banner*, 1 December 1937, 11; and "'Moon Maiden' Matinee Today," *The Duncan Banner*, 2 December 1937, 6.

In April, the Duncan choral groups placed sixth in their district. The combined choral and instrumental and solo and small ensemble scores yielded a seventh place for the school. At the state finals in Stillwater in May, none of the Duncan solos, ensembles, or large groups earned a Superior or Excellent rating.[15]

Leonhard communicated his ideas about the future of the music department early in his first year. At a meeting of the school board in October, he described his job as a four-fold responsibility: senior high school music theory, junior high general music, large vocal groups, and small vocal groups. His first semester plans for the Duncan vocal music department also included a junior high school operetta to be given in the late fall, a senior high operetta to be given in the spring, and annual music contests at Durant and Norman.[16]

As he remembered the program in later years, Leonhard inherited a rather weak situation. The high school choral program was in a decidedly run down condition, and so one of his first tasks was to increase the enrollment. This he managed to do quite successfully. In his second year at Duncan, he had sixty students in a boys' glee club, and he had a mixed chorus and a girls' glee club.[17]

In the fall of 1938, Leonhard added the position of Supervisor of Elementary School Music to his responsibilities. This entailed his working with elementary music teachers, giving assistance, doing workshops, and—where necessary—providing teachers with lesson plans. He worked at the high school in the mornings and

---

[15]"Oklahoma Interscholastic Music Contest," *Oklahoma Agricultural and Mechanical College Bulletin* (December 1938): 46, 51–52.

[16]"Tenors Scarce at Duncan High."

[17]Leonhard interview, 13 October 1990.

did his supervisory work with the elementary music teachers in the afternoons.[18]

In the spring of 1939, Leonhard's students went to the district contest in Oklahoma City. Of the thirty-eight schools taking apart in the contest there, the Duncan choral groups placed sixteenth. The school placed eighth, overall, thanks to a strong showing from the instrumental department. No choral solos, ensembles, or large groups received superior or excellent ratings at the state contest in Norman in 1939. In 1940 and 1941, the instrumental groups from Duncan High School participated in the contests, but Leonhard's choral groups did not.[19]

In Leonhard's last year in Duncan, the high school had a faculty of twenty-eight. The school had three grades in which were enrolled 110 seniors, 89 juniors, and 70 sophomores. These declining numbers suggest a deteriorating economic situation in the community. Leonhard began thinking about seeking employment in a place where he could earn more money and enjoy greater prestige, as well as have a greater challenge than the position in Duncan provided. Nevertheless, his program there was a full one.[20]

In 1940–41, 125 students participated in vocal music activities at Duncan High. These included mixed chorus, girls' glee club, boys' quartet, and girls' quartet. The groups put on a concert in December of 1940 and participated in the commencement activities in the spring of

[18]Leonhard to Heller, 1 January 1989; Leonhard interview, 13 October 1990; and Leonhard to Heller 17 May 1993.

[19]"Oklahoma Interscholastic Music Contest," *University of Oklahoma Bulletin*, 6 November 1939, pp. 40–41, 44–45; "National School Music Competition Festivals," *Oklahoma Agricultural and Mechanical College Bulletin*, March 1941, pp. 72–73, 77–78; and *National School Music Competition-Festivals: 1941 Reports* (Chicago: National School Band, Orchestra and Vocal Associations, 1941), 36–37, 41–44, 75.

[20]*Demon Round-Up* (1941), pp. 10–12, 15–22, 25–30, 33–36; and Leonhard to Heller, 17 May 1993.

## Figure 9

Charles Leonhard, Duncan High School Faculty, 1941*

*Demon Round-Up* (1941), 11.

1941. In addition, they performed an operetta and a cantata in alternate years. During the 1940–41 school year, Leonhard began a music club, called the B. B. B. Club. The initials stood for Bach, Beethoven, and Brahms. Members of the group met during home room, where they sang and listened to music. Leonhard later remembered that he had founded the club as "a way of consolidating interest in music and getting students who were really interested in music in a sharper focus."[21] It had thirty members in its first year.[22]

At the end of his first year of teaching in Duncan, Leonhard went to New York City to enroll in the graduate program in music education at Teachers College, Columbia University. His piano teacher, Lois Bennett, had persuaded him to go to Teachers College. For many years, she had spent her summers in New York taking courses at Teachers College and at The Juilliard School, then located nearby in Morningside Heights. "During the year I would from time to time go to Chickasha to see and have a lesson with Miss Bennett. She encouraged me to begin a master's degree at Teachers College and I took her advice to go there in June of 1938."[23] That first summer he enrolled in Conducting and Score Reading with Norval L. Church, Physical Basis of Music (Acoustics), and Teaching Music in the Intermediate Grades with one of Dykema's graduate assistants.[24]

Teachers College in the 1930s was something of a mecca for music educators, especially those who were interested in graduate work. Peter W. Dykema (1873–1951) was chair of music education there, a position he had held since 1924. Dykema retired in 1940 at the end of a career that had seen him chair the music department at the

[21] Leonhard interview, 13 October 1990.

[22] *Demon Round-Up* (1941), 39–44, 82.

[23] Leonhard to Heller, 8 June 1989.

[24] Leonhard interview, 13 October 1990.

Figure 10

The Duncan High School Girls' Quartet*

*Demon Round-Up* (1941), 44.

University of Wisconsin, preside over the Music
Supervisors National Conference, and serve as the first
editor of the *Music Supervisors Journal* (1914–21).
Dykema had made something of a name for himself as a
leader in the community song movement and as editor of
the *Twice 55 Community Song Book*, published in
various editions from 1919 to 1927. He and Church
published a band method book in 1939.[25]

While Leonhard was at Teachers College, Dykema
offered a course in aesthetics. Since it was not a required
course, Leonhard did not take it. "My contact with Dykema
was principally through the very active program of [Phi Mu
Alpha] Sinfonia of which Dykema was a founder. Teachers
College had a very large and active chapter of Sinfonia and
Dykema, having written the ritual, was usually high priest at
the initiation. I also came under his influence as a director of
community singing at which he was a master."[26]

Despite his interest in public school music and choral
directing, Leonhard still held to his ambitions at the
keyboard. In the summer of 1938, he had saved up enough
money to study privately with Harold Bauer in New York.
". . . I made contact with Harold Bauer who was at that time
one of the top American concert pianists and gave instruction
in piano in his studio in New York. Private lessons with
Mr. Bauer were fifty dollars for a half hour which at that
time was a tremendous amount of money."[27] With the
increase in salary Mr. George had given him and the added
income from piano lessons, Leonhard managed to save up

[25]The definitive study on Dykema is Henry E. Eisenkramer, "Peter
William Dykema: His Life and Contribution to Music Education" (Ed.D.
diss., Teachers College, Columbia University, 1963). For a brief summary,
see *The New Grove Dictionary of American Music*, 1986 ed., s.v. "Dykema,
Peter W.," by George N. Heller.

[26]Leonhard to Heller, 8 June 1989.

[27]Ibid.

three hundred dollars for lessons with Bauer during the summer of 1938.

Harold Bauer (1873–1951) was born in London and came to the United States for the first time on a concert tour in 1900. He moved permanently to the U. S. in 1918 and promoted performances of chamber music in New York City. He specialized in solo and chamber works of the late romantics and impressionist composers.[28]

Bauer let the young school teacher from Oklahoma down easy, when, after one lesson, he suggested that Leonhard might better profit from taking Bauer's master class for a much smaller fee than the more expensive private lessons in his studio. "As a result, I attended his master classes twice a week throughout the summer."[29]

Leonhard's first summer in the Big Apple offered more than attending classes and taking lessons. The World's Fair was on in the summer of 1938. Leonhard and his colleagues spent time at the extravaganza, called the World of Tomorrow. Leonhard remembered it as "really an eye-opener for a young man from the Sooner State. Several of my friends and I went to the fair a number of times in both the summer of 1938 and its continuation during the summer of 1939."[30] These summers also provided the young Oklahoman with his first opportunity to hear big city orchestral music. "The New York Philharmonic played at Lewisohn Stadium which was north of Morningside Heights and I went there regularly."[31]

Leonhard's second summer at Teachers College was a full one. He took Chromatic Harmony, Composition, and Analysis with Helen Budge. He also enrolled in another

[28]*The New Grove Dictionary of American Music*, 1986 ed., s.v. "Bauer, Harold," by H. C. Colles and Ronald Kinloch Anderson.

[29]Leonhard to Heller, 8 June 1989.

[30]Ibid.

[31]Ibid.

theory course called Composition and Analysis which Howard Murphy taught. In addition to these courses in music theory, Leonhard also took Teaching Piano to Adults with Raymond Burrows, Teaching Voice Culture with Harry Robert Wilson, Dalcroze Eurhythmics, and Choral Methods and Materials with Carl Gutekunst.[32]

It was rather common practice at Teachers College to have visiting instructors from around the country. Among the ones Leonhard was privileged to study with was Peter Tkach of Minneapolis. "He came to Teachers College one summer to conduct the Teachers College chorus, and I sang under him and learned a great deal about choral conducting and choral rehearsals."[33]

Howard A. Murphy (1896–1962) taught at Teachers College from 1927 until his retirement in 1961. He took his ideas about music theory from George Wedge and Percy Goetschius. He developed his own ideas about teaching from his associations with James L. Mursell and Norval Church at Teachers College and from other theorists and professional associations. No doubt Murphy's own graduate students also had some affect on him. He served as the first chair of the Music Educators National Conference Committee on Contemporary Music from 1941 through 1946. Leonhard called Murphy "My most notable contact at Teachers College. . . . I took several courses with Murphy in Musicianship and Counterpoint along with a course in Contemporary Music."[34]

In the summer of 1940, Leonhard studied Principles, Practices, and Materials in Music Education with Lilla Belle

[32]Leonhard Interview, 13 October 1990.

[33]Leonhard to Heller, 8 June 1989; and Leonhard interview, 13 October 1990.

[34]Leonhard to Heller, 8 June 1989. See also Richard N. Olsen, "Howard A. Murphy, Theorist and Teacher: His Influence on the Teaching of Basic Music Theory in American Colleges and Universities from 1940 to 1973," Ed.D. diss., University of Illinois, 1973.

Pitts. He continued his music theory training with Fundamentals of Music II and Teaching Theory of Music, both from Murphy.[35]

This was the first meeting in what was to become a long-time association between Leonhard and Lilla Belle Pitts (1884–1970). Pitts was a veteran school music teacher before joining the faculty at Teachers College in 1938. She had taken her bachelors degree there in 1935 and was a student of Charles Farnsworth and Dykema. She was president of the Music Educators National Conference (1942–44) and edited school music textbooks for Ginn and Company in the 1940s and 1950s.[36]

In the summer of 1940, Leonhard also took a course in "Extra-Curricular Activities," at the behest of his superintendent in Duncan. "The person who initiated the idea about homerooms was on the faculty at Teachers College, and he gave this course in extracurricular activities. And [Norval] George wanted to start that at Duncan. He requested that I take this course with—I forget his name, Carswell, I think. He was the originator of the homeroom idea."[37]

In the summer of 1941, Leonhard ventured into the education courses for which Teachers College was famous. In that year, he took Educational Foundations (200FA). This was one of a series of courses in the history and philosophy of education offered by such luminaries as Harold O. Rugg, George S. Counts, Foster McMurray, and John L. Childs.[38]

[35]Leonhard to Heller, 8 June 1989.

[36]Gerald L. Blanchard, "Lilla Belle Pitts: Her Life and Contribution to Music Education" (Ed.D. diss., Brigham Young University, 1966); and *The New Grove Dictionary of American Music*, 1986 ed., s.v. "Pitts, Lilla Belle," by George N. Heller.

[37]Leonhard interview, 13 October 1990.

[38]Leonhard, Teachers College Transcript.

Rugg was a leading progressive educator who wrote in the areas of social science, research, and statistics. Counts was an educational sociologist who was also active in politics as the New York State Chair of the American Labor Party and the American Civil Liberties Union. In the years Leonhard studied with him, Counts was president of the American Federation of Teachers (1939–42). McMurray is known to music educators for his article on pragmatism in music education in the 1958 yearbook of the National Society for the Study of Education. Childs taught philosophy of education with a pragmatist bent. Among his better known books were *Education and the Philosophy of Experimentalism* (1931); *America, Russia, and the Communist Party* (with George Counts, 1943); and *American Pragmatism and Education* (1956).[39]

Leonhard credits these professors of educational foundations at Teacher College with developing his ideas about socialism and populism. He was entranced by the lectures and panel discussions these men gave, and their courses also provided him with his first meaningful contact with the ideas of John Dewey, which would in turn affect his own approach to the foundations of music education.[40]

During the summer of 1941, Leonhard also enrolled in Advanced Voice Class and in James L. Mursell's Psychological Foundations of Music Education. Mursell, recently arrived on the scene at Teachers College, was to

[39]*Biographical Dictionary of American Educators*, 1978 ed., s.v. "Rugg, Harold Ordway," by Murray R. Nelson, and "Counts, George Sylvester," by Ralph E. Ackerman; Foster McMurray, "Pragmatism in Music Education," in *Basic Concepts in Music Education*, ed. Nelson B. Henry (Chicago: National Society for the Study of Education, 1958), 30–61; June Edwards, "Indoctrination into Freedom: John Childs Speaks for Today," *Contemporary Education* 58 (Fall 1986): 18–21; and William Van Til, "John L. Childs: An Appreciation," *Contemporary Education* 58 (Fall 1986): 21.

[40]Leonhard to Heller, 1 January 1989.

influence Leonhard greatly in his doctoral studies after the war and throughout his career.[41]

James Lockhart Mursell (1893–1963) was born in England and educated there and in Australia before taking his Ph.D. at Harvard in 1918. After a brief career as a church minister, he went to Lawrence College (now University) in Appleton, Wisconsin, where he taught from 1923–35. Mursell joined the staff at Teachers College in 1935 and succeeded Peter Dykema as chair of music education in 1940. He remained in that position until 1957.[42]

Mursell had completed two major works on educational psychology in 1939, just two years before Leonhard took his course on the psychological foundations of music education in the summer of 1941. Two years later, in 1943, Silver Burdett published Mursell's *Music in American Schools*. No doubt these works had a major impact on Leonhard as he set about to articulate his own ideas on music education.[43]

Leonhard completed all the requirements and thereby earned the Master of Arts Degree in Music Education. Teachers College awarded his degree on December 17,

[41]Leonhard, Teachers College Transcript, and Leonhard interview, 13 October 1990.

[42]Three thorough studies of Mursell's life and works are Leonard J. Simutis, "James L. Mursell as Music Educator" (Ph.D. diss., University of Ottawa, 1961); Donald E. Metz, "A Critical Analysis of the Thought of James L. Mursell in Music Education" (Ph.D. diss., Case Western Reserve University, 1968); and Vincent C. O'Keefe, "James Lockhart Mursell, His Life and Contributions to Music Education" (Ed.D. diss., Teachers College, Columbia University, 1970). For a shorter summary, see *The New Grove Dictionary of American Music*, 1986 ed., s.v. "Mursell, James L(ockhart)," by George N. Heller.

[43]The two textbooks were James L. Mursell, *Educational Psychology* (New York: W. W. Norton & Company, Inc., 1939) and James L, Mursell, *The Psychology of Secondary-School Teaching* (New York: W. W. Norton & Company, Inc., 1939). See Leonard J. Simutis, "James L. Mursell: An Annotated Bibliography," *Journal of Research in Music Education* 16 (Fall 1968): 254–266. One of Mursell's most influential early works was James L. Mursell and Mabelle Glenn, *The Psychology of School Music Teaching* (New York: Silver Burdett Company, 1931). He revised this book in 1938.

1941, just ten days after the attack on Pearl Harbor by the Japanese which signalled the beginning of World War II.[44]

Taking a master's degree in summers at Teachers College in New York City was something of a revelation for Leonhard, and it served as a transition for him from the comfortable pace of life in the Midwest to the faster tempo of the east coast and especially the big city. "These years [19]38–41 gave me my first taste of Broadway including Tallulah Bankhead in the 'Little Foxes' and Marlon Brando in 'A Streetcar Named Desire.'"[45]

Leonhard's life in New York included unique musical experiences as well. He sang in the St. Paul's Chapel Choir at Columbia under the direction of Charles Doersam. "I became entranced with ritual for the first time in the high church service at St. Paul's. We were paid, 16 selected singers, with money that came from interest on an endowment that King George III had given to King's College to support a chapel service at 7:00 a.m. each weekday and at 11:00 a.m on Sunday."[46]

Leonhard felt quite at home taking summer courses at Teachers College. Many of his fellow students were Midwesterners, there being only a handful of other schools around the country where one could do graduate work in music education at that time. About eighty percent of the students he attended classes with were women, which essentially reflected the profession at that time. He met many people during his years there and developed life-long friendships with many of them, though he regarded them more for their personal qualities than their professional acumen. "During this period I developed both casual and intimate friendships, some of which have lasted over the 50

[44]Leonhard, Teachers College transcript.

[45]Leonhard to Heller, 1 January 1989.

[46]Ibid.

year period. None of the students I knew at Teachers
College at that time ever really made big names in music
education, but all of them did yeoman service in their various
schools throughout the country."[47]

Not foreseeing the cataclysmic events of the coming
year, Leonhard decided to advance his career by moving on
from Duncan, Oklahoma to the growing metropolis of
Dallas, Texas. In the spring of 1941, he had gone to Dallas
to attend some Metropolitan Opera performances. Marion E.
Flagg (1894–1968) was also a graduate of Teacher College
and a student of Dykema, Pitts, and Mursell. She had
recently (in 1940) joined the Dallas schools as Director of
Music, succeeding Sudie Williams. While in town for the
opera, Leonhard made an appointment to see Miss Flagg and
to talk about a teaching position in the Dallas schools. "She
gave me an appointment, and I went to see her at the Board
of Education. She put me through my paces; had me do
absolutely everything. She had me play a piano solo, sing a
solo, read music at sight, sight-sing, read and play an octavo
score, and then we talked about music education. And so
that represented the interview. And the next week I got a
contact from Dallas."[48]

Leonhard took a position as choral director of two
Dallas high schools in the fall of 1941. He worked at the
Woodrow Wilson High School in a well-to-do
neighborhood on the east side of Dallas and at Adamson
High School in an industrial area west of the Trinity River in
Oak Cliff. The Dallas Schools were segregated at that time,

---

[47]Leonhard to Heller, 1 January 1989; and Leonhard to Heller, 17
May 1993.

[48]Leonhard interview, 13 October 1990. Flagg earned a bachelor's
degree at Teachers College in 1929 and a master's there in 1932. From
1926 to 1939, she was on the faculty of the Horace Mann Laboratory
School. For more on Ms. Flagg, see Carole J. Delaney, "The Contribution
of Marion Flagg to Music and Education" (D.M.A. diss., The University of
Texas, 1974).

and both schools Leonhard worked in had no African-American students. His salary was $1,800 for the year.[49]

Two events in Leonhard's brief career in Dallas solidified his reputation with both Miss Flagg and the Superintendent, Walter White. One of these was a Teachers Convocation at which Leonhard led 1,200 teachers in a very successful singing of "America the Beautiful." He had twenty of his best sopranos from Adamson High School back stage, and he had them step out from behind the curtain to sing the Dykema descant for the second verse. He also organized the first boys' glee club at Adamson. The local radio station invited the sixty-five voice choir to sing a thirty-minute program of Christmas songs live on December 7, 1941. White was so impressed with Leonhard's work that he kept him on leave for the duration of the war and sent him a contract every year until he formally resigned in 1950.[50]

Flagg apparently cultivated an awareness in Leonhard of the intellectual side of music teaching. During his brief time in Dallas, and probably prompted by his experiences at Teachers College, he began to ask questions and formulate opinions about the meaning and value of teaching music in the schools. Flagg apparently supported this. ". . . I had a close relationship with Marion Flagg who was Director of Music. She helped me realize how damned smart I am and gave me my first experience in intellectualizing the processes of music education."[51]

At this time of his life, Leonhard also had some serious encounters with religious issues. He joined the Christian Science Church in Dallas and practiced it faithfully for two years. In later years, he reflected on the experience as

---

[49]Leonhard to Heller, 1 January 1989; and Kritzmire, "The Pedagogy of Charles Leonhard," 57.

[50]Leonhard to Heller, 17 May 1993.

[51]Leonhard to Heller, 1 January 1989.

having changed his attitude toward his physical well-being and toward illness which he retained even after giving up the formal practice of Christian Science. Following his encounter with Christian Science in Dallas in 1941, Leonhard has thought of himself as a "born again atheist [ever] since."[52]

Leonhard came to grips with the infinite just in time to face the possibility of joining it. During his first year of teaching in the Dallas schools, the Japanese attacked Pearl Harbor, and Congress declared war on the Axis powers and Japan. It was just a matter of time before the former ROTC student became a soldier on active duty. Leonhard took a military leave of absence from his teaching position in Dallas and entered the service on March 9, 1942. The Army assigned Leonhard a service number, 0 355 491, and sent him to Fort Sill, Oklahoma for training in the Battery Officers Course. After completing the course in one month, he went to Camp Barclay, Texas, where he served with the headquarters battery of the 90th Division.[53]

Having been commissioned a Second Lieutenant in 1937 on completion of his ROTC training, Leonhard was the senior lieutenant in the battery and thus became battery commander with the rank of First Lieutenant. By September of 1942, Leonhard had attained the rank of Captain, and went to Camp Van Dorn, Mississippi, as Commanding Officer of the Headquarters Battery of the 371st Field Artillery Battalion of the 99th Division. He went overseas as commander of the Headquarters Battery, 757th Field Artillery Battalion on August 22, 1944 and saw service in New Guinea (September), New Britain (October and November), and the Admiralty Islands (December). He

---

[52]Leonhard to Heller, 1 January 1989.

[53]Ibid.; Kritzmire, "The Pedagogy of Charles Leonhard," 58–59; and Charles Leonhard, Urbana, IL, to George N. Heller, Lawrence, KS, 1 June 1993, original in possession of the author.

participated in the invasion of Luzon, Philippine Islands on January 9, 1945.[54]

Leonhard felt that he gained command experience and developed administrative and human relations abilities in his military service. He seemed to relate easily to both enlisted men under his command and officers who were peers or superiors. "The Army really transformed me and my life. Those years were in many respects the happiest and most rewarding of my life, and what I learned to do and what I became as a result of the army years stood me in good stead in my professional career."[55]

The war turned around in mid-1944, with the invasion of Europe on D-Day, June 6. Less than a year later, the allies declared V-E (Victory in Europe) Day on May 2, 1945. That summer, the United States dropped atomic bombs on Japan (August 6 and August 9, 1945), and on August 14, 1945, Japan surrendered.

Leonhard was in the Philippines at war's end. Since he was not married, he was not immediately mustered out of the army. Rather, the Army assigned him to the Information and Education Section of the Southwest Pacific Armed Forces Command. There he attained a promotion to the rank of Major in July of 1945 and worked at organizing classes for soldiers who were also waiting orders to return to the United States for their discharge from the war. Despite the scaling down of the Army, Leonhard's superiors offered him another promotion in rank if he would stay on active duty. Leonhard declined, having better things in mind for his life. "I was offered a promotion to Lt. Colonel if I would stay in the army, but I really did not like the

---

[54]Leonhard to Heller, 17 May 1993; and John Costello, *The Pacific War* (New York: Rawson, Wade, 1981), 531–534.

[55]Leonhard to Heller, 1 January 1989.

aimlessness of the peace time army as I had experienced it in Manilla from August 1945 to March 1946."[56]

Leonhard considered his time in the army a rewarding experience, one that would serve him well in later years. "I learned during my Army service how important it is to have definite objectives. . . . I learned for the first time the breadth of my abilities, that I wasn't limited to playing the piano or conducting a choral group, that I had a whole wide range of abilities that I had never made use of."[57] In the service Leonhard had assumed major administrative responsibilities under very critical and stressful circumstances. He learned that he could handle these kinds of situations very well.

And so the Oklahoma warrior came home; he was discharged at Fort Leavenworth, Kansas on May 16, 1946. To put into play all that he had experienced in his public school teaching and all that he had gained from his military service, Leonhard headed for his next stop: Teachers College, Columbia University, New York City.[58]

[56]Leonhard to Heller, 1 January 1989. See also Leonhard to Heller, 1 June 1993.

[57]Leonhard interview, 13 October 1990.

[58]Charles Leonhard, Discharge papers, U. S. Army, 16 May 1946, photocopy in possession of the author.

# CHAPTER III

# DOCTORAL STUDENT
# AND COLLEGE PROFESSOR

Leonhard left the army with a substantial nest egg of back pay and savings. With this, he headed for New York City and the doctoral program in music education at Teachers College, Columbia University. Because of Leonhard's success there earlier, Howard Murphy, among others, had encouraged him to return to Teachers College and join the faculty. It was here, from 1946 to 1951, that Leonhard learned to live, work, and succeed in higher education. During these five years he led a very full life teaching classes, meeting leaders in the field, beginning his publishing career, and earning his doctorate.[1]

Being single and fairly affluent, Leonhard had an active social life in the city. He had season tickets to the Metropolitan Opera and he went to and sometimes served as the co-host at dinners for singers from the Met. He attended New York Philharmonic concerts on a regular basis and often had invitations to opening nights on Broadway. "I tasted everything that New York had to offer, both sacred and profane, and lived life in the fast lane. A truly memorable five years for a farm boy from Oklahoma."[2]

---

[1]Leonhard to Heller, 8 June 1989.

[2]Leonhard to Heller, 1 January 1989.

Leonhard enrolled at Teachers College in the summer session of 1946. He was a student in the doctoral program and held a full-time position at the rank of instructor. That summer he took but one class, 200FB, Education as Personal Development, taught by Goodwin Watson (1899-1976). While not world famous for its course offerings in music, Teachers College did have a stable full of thoroughbreds in educational theory and foundations. In addition to Harold O. Rugg, George S. Counts, and John L. Childs, with whom Leonhard studied in his master's program, the faculty included the eminent educational psychologist, Goodwin B. Watson. Watson taught at Teachers College from 1925 to 1962, and he wrote on religious education, objective assessment of character and personality, education in the Soviet Union, and social change.[3]

Leonhard made his first contact with Susanne K. Langer (1895–1985) when he enrolled in her Seminar and Project in Music and Art in the fall term of 1946. It was a seminar with thirteen other graduate students. The Rockefeller Foundation funded the seminar which required Langer to be in residence at Teachers College.[4]

Langer was a significant American philosopher who was concerned with developing a theory of musical meaning. This in turn led her to a philosophy of art and a general philosophy of the mind. Her major works were current when Leonhard was in New York and in the years soon afterward. Of Langer, Leonhard later recalled that she "opened up new horizons on the nature of symbolism, its

---

[3]Jeanne Watson Eisenstadt, "Remembering Goodwin Watson," *Journal of Social Issues* 42 (1986): 49–52; and "Dr. Goodwin Watson, Taught at Columbia," *New York Times* 5 January 1977, B 18.

[4]Kritzmire, "The Pedagogy of Charles Leonhard," 74.

importance in the feelingful life of all human beings, and its pertinence to aesthetic education."[5]

In addition to Langer's seminar, Leonhard took courses in Counterpoint, Trends in Contemporary Music, and Analysis in Relation to Hearing and Performance, all with Murphy. Murphy continued to be his mentor in the doctoral program as he had been in the master's program. It was through Murphy's contacts and influence that Leonhard became associated with Henry Cowell, who at that time was involved with advancing the cause of contemporary music at the New School for Social Research and in the Composer's Forum in New York.[6]

Leonhard and Murphy worked very closely at Teachers College. The two had what could be described as a student-mentor relationship. Leonhard later commented that Murphy "not only gave me my start as a music theorist and teacher of music theory; he consistently guided me with expert counsel. We had a personal and professional relationship that was truly inspiring. He introduced me to Henry Cowell and Alan McHose, the Eastman theorist, both of whom influenced my thinking about contemporary music and the teaching of theory."[7]

---

[5]Charles Leonhard, Urbana, IL, to George N. Heller, Lawrence, KS, 9 June 1993. Langer's publications include *Philosophy in a New Key* (Cambridge, MA: Harvard University Press, 1942, rev. 1951); *Feeling and Form* (New York: Charles Scribner's Sons, 1953), and *Problems of Art* (New York: Charles Scribner's Sons, 1957). See *The New Grove Dictionary of American Music*, 1986 ed., s.v. "Langer, Susanne K.," by F. E. Sparshott and Paula Morgan; and Ethel M. Kersey, *Women Philosophers: A Biocritical Source Book* (New York: Greenwood Press, 1989), s.v. "Langer, Susanne Katherina Knauth."

[6]Leonhard interview, 13 October 1990. On Cowell, see *The New Grove Dictionary of American Music*, 1986 ed., s.v. "Cowell, Henry (Dixon)," by Bruce Saylor, William Lichtenwanger, and Elizabeth A. Wright; and Rita H. Mead, "The Amazing Mr. Cowell," *American Music* 1 (Winter 1983): 63–89. Murphy was a member of the National Association for American Composers and Conductors, a group in New York City which promoted contemporary American music. He may have met Cowell through that organization.

[7]Leonhard to Heller, 9 June 1993.

As if he did not have enough to do, Leonhard studied piano for credit with Raymond Burrows in that first fall semester back at Teachers College after the war. He also found time to take private piano lessons with Tom Richner, a member of the piano faculty at Teachers College.[8]

Teachers College in the late forties and early fifties was inundated by veterans returning from World War II. These students enjoyed generous support from the federal government to begin or—as was the case with Leonhard—to continue their higher education. The school, while renowned for its faculty and courses in music education, was not particularly strong in music. However, Teachers College did have the advantage of being located very near The Juilliard School which then as now had a very fine program in music performance and composition.[9]

In the spring term of 1947 Leonhard took another full load, including Counterpoint with Murphy and Analysis in Relation to Hearing and Performance with Adele Katz. He studied piano with Burrows again, Seminar and Project in Music with Langer, and Design and Style in Music with Murphy.[10]

While taking all this course work in music and music education, Leonhard met Vanett Lawler (1902–1970). Lilla Belle Pitts introduced Leonhard to Lawler during his first full year in the doctoral program. This was the beginning of his long-time association with the Music Educators National Conference.[11]

---

[8]Leonhard transcript.

[9]Letter from Lewis B. Hilton, St. Louis, MO, to George N. Heller, Lawrence, KS, 3 February 1990.

[10]Leonhard interview, 13 October 1990; and Leonhard to Heller, 9 June 1993.

[11]Leonhard interview, 13 October 1990; and Leonhard to Heller, 1 January 1989.

When Leonhard studied with Pitts before the war, she had been a junior high school general music teacher in the public schools of Elizabeth, New Jersey, and a part-time member of the music education faculty at Teachers College. While Leonhard was in the service, Pitts had attained national stature, culminating in her election to the presidency of the Music Educators National Conference in 1942. She served in that capacity until 1944. After the war, she became involved in writing and editing elementary and junior high school music textbooks. At the time Leonhard studied with her in the late 1940s, she was working on a series, Our Singing World, for Ginn and Company.[12]

Pitts was also a kind of mentor to Leonhard and helped get him involved in many aspects of music education not ordinarily available to most people. In addition to introducing him to Ms. Lawler and the MENC, Lilla Belle also introduced him to the world of general music series book publishing. Four of his songs are included in the Ginn series, which Pitts edited along with Mabelle Glenn, Lorrain E. Watters, and Louis G. Wersen. The series first came out in 1949, and it was slightly revised in 1957.[13]

Leonhard's contributions to the Ginn series were as follows: "Shoe the Horse," a setting of a nursery rhyme text, appeared in *Singing on Our Way* (second grade book, 1949, 1957, p. 132); "Jack Frost," text by Helen B. Davis, in *Singing Every Day* (fourth grade book, 1950, 1957, p. 136); "I Heard It in the Valley," text by Annette Wynne, in *Singing Together* (fifth grade book, 1951, 1957, p. 158); and "Afternoon on a Hill," text by Edna St. Vincent Millay, in *Singing in Harmony* (sixth grade book, 1951, 1957, p.

[12]Blanchard, "Lilla Belle Pitts"; *The New Grove Dictionary of American Music*, 1986 ed., s.v. "Pitts, Lilla Belle," by George N. Heller; and Leonhard to Heller, 9 June 1993.

[13]Lilla Belle Pitts, Mabelle Glenn, Lorrain E. Watters, and Louis G. Wersen, Our Singing World, 9 vols. [Kindergarten through eighth grade] (Boston: Ginn and Company, 1949–1957).

## Figure 11

## "Afternoon on a Hill"*

Afternoon on a Hill

Edna St. Vincent Millay

*Expressively*

Charles Leonhard

166

*From *Singing in Harmony* of Our Singing World series, ©
Copyright, 1959, 1957, 1951, by Ginn and company. Used by permission
of Silver Burdett Ginn Inc.

166). Leonhard wrote a piano accompaniment part for "Afternoon on a Hill"; the others are unaccompanied melodies suitable for children's voices.

In addition to working on her series for Ginn, Pitts maintained a close relationship with the Music Educators National Conference, and particularly with Vanett Lawler. Lawler was from Minnesota, where she had studied piano. She graduated from the University of Wisconsin in 1924 with a degree in business. Her first few jobs were with commercial firms as an advertising and marketing specialist. In 1930 she joined the newly opened executive office of the Music Supervisors National Conference (which became the Music Educators National Conference in 1934) in Chicago as assistant to Clifford V. Buttelman. She succeeded Buttelman as executive secretary of the Conference in 1953 and remained in that position until her retirement in 1968.[14]

Leonhard reflected in later years that Ms. Pitts had a strong personal and professional influence on him. She encouraged the young doctoral student to get involved in the Music Educators National Conference, she introduced him to school music publishing, and she saw to it that he participated in many of the cultural activities that New York City had to offer. "She gave me entrée into the worlds of the MENC, publishing, and the Metropolitan Opera by introducing me to a host of her friends and associates including Vanett Lawler, Henry Halvorson, music editor at Ginn and Company, and Blanche Witherspoon, Executive Director of the Metropolitan Opera Guild."[15]

In the fall of 1947, Leonhard plunged once again into a full regimen of courses. He took American Pragmatism and Education with John Childs, and studied Teaching and

---

[14]Christy Izdebski and Michael L. Mark, "Vanett Lawler: International Music Education Administrator," *The Bulletin of Historical Research in Music Education* 8 (January 1987): 1–32.

[15]Leonhard to Heller, 9 June 1993

Supervision of Music in Primary Grades with Pitts. He also took Advanced Piano Instruction with Burrows.[16]

In the spring of 1948 Leonhard took Teaching and Supervision of Music in Intermediate Grades with Pitts. He studied Education and Creative America, 1860s–1940s with Harold Rugg, and took a course in Organization and Functioning of Instruction of Higher Education with Edward S. Evenden. That summer he enrolled in Psychology of Adolescence with Goodwin Watson.[17]

In his final year as a student at Teachers College, in addition to writing his dissertation, Leonhard took a general course in Mental Hygiene for Teachers. He also had a course in Principles of Teaching and another in Educational Psychology and Its Application to Music, both with Mursell, in the fall of 1948.[18]

In the spring of 1949, Leonhard took Education in the Democratic State with John Childs and General Course in Curriculum Development with Alice Miel. He also took voice lessons and studied piano again with Burrows. Upon completing all of his course work and defending his dissertation, Leonhard earned the Ed.D. degree from Teachers College on June 1, 1949.[19]

While taking all these courses and teaching what amounted to a full-time load, Leonhard also studied privately with Julius Herford (1901–1981), though not for credit. Herford had been on the faculty at Teachers College from 1939–41. After the war he was at the Juilliard School (1946–64), the Berkshire Music Center (1946–64), the

[16]Leonhard interview, 13 October 1990.

[17]Leonhard, Teachers College Transcript.

[18]Leonhard interview, 13 October 1990.

[19]Dwight D. Eisenhower, then president of Columbia University, signed Leonhard's diploma. See Charles Leonhard, Diploma, Doctor of Education, Teachers College, Columbia University, 1 June 1949, photocopy in possession of the author.

Union Theological Seminary (1949–64), and the Manhattan School of Music (1949–64). Herford was a prolific writer, turning out many books and articles on music education. He was also a composer of choral works. Among his students were Robert Shaw, Lukas Foss, and Roger Wagner.[20]

Leonhard had a responsibility to teach a course in counterpoint. He and Howard Murphy had taken turns teaching this course. Leonhard knew of Herford and the work he was doing with Robert Shaw, and sought him out to gain a new perspective on the teaching of counterpoint. They made arrangements for Leonhard to take weekly lessons at Herford's New York apartment, but they never really got around to studying counterpoint, per se. Rather, Herford had Leonhard buy the Dessoff Choir Series, and these served as the basis for the lessons. "So what we did for four hours once a week for a year was to take these various pieces of Renaissance choral music and sing and play through them and then analyze them for style. Perfectly marvelous!"[21]

Julius Herford was a great inspiration to Leonhard. Leonhard admired Herford's "keen insight into the structure of music and its implications for revealing the expressive import of music." Leonhard later said that his study with Herford "revolutionized my approach to the analysis and interpretation of music."[22]

Leonhard's doctoral dissertation was entitled, "A Study of the Teaching of Transposition at the Piano by the Use of the Seven Clefs." Howard A. Murphy served as major advisor, and Norval L. Church and James L. Mursell were on the committee. The dissertation, called "A Report

---

[20]*The New Grove Dictionary of American Music*, 1986 ed., s.v. "Herford, Julius." See also Leonhard to Heller, 1 January 1989.

[21]Leonhard interview, 13 October 1990. See also Leonhard to Heller, 9 June 1993.

[22]Leonhard to Heller, 9 June 1993.

of a Type A Project," was approved by that committee in partial fulfillment of the requirements for the degree of Doctor of Education in the Advanced School of Education, Teachers College, Columbia University on May 10, 1949.[23]

The dissertation is an eighty-four page document consisting of an introduction, a history of the experimental course at Teachers College, a discussion of the technique used in that course, a description of materials, practices and procedures, case studies with comments by students, and a one-page statement of conclusions. This is followed by a one page booklist, a fifty-one page course of study, and a two-page summary. Appendices showing examples (three pages) and chorales used (three pages) and a one-page bibliography complete the document.

The study reported the work of a music theory class in the function of chromatic harmony offered at Teachers College in 1947–48. All eight students in the course had considerable piano proficiency, and "registration was limited to a small and select group of students. There were included a professional accompanist, a staff pianist for a radio station, a voice teacher, and several teachers of public school music."[24] Of the eight students enrolled, six passed the course and two failed.

At the conclusion of the course, Leonhard asked students to make statements about what they had experienced. He published six of these in his report. Five of the students were fairly laudatory of the program, its goals, and its methods. One, however, was not. "Miss F. was a person of below average intelligence, but with an excellent ear and considerable musical talent. Her piano facility was mediocre and her theory background inadequate.

[23]Charles Leonhard, "A Study of the Teaching of Transposition at the Piano by the Use of the Seven Clefs" (Ed.D. diss., Teachers College, Columbia University, 1949). An abstract of Leonhard's dissertation appears in *Teachers College Record* 52 (October 1950): 59–60.

[24]Leonhard, "A Study of the Teaching of Transposition," 5.

Figure 12

Title Page of Leonhard's Doctoral Dissertation

A STUDY OF THE TEACHING OF TRANSPOSITION AT THE PIANO

BY THE USE OF THE SEVEN CLEFS

A Report of a Type A Project

by

CHARLES LEONHARD

This project is recommended for approval by the Student's Project
Committee whose individual certificates of approval are on file in
the Advanced School
                              N. L. Church, Member of Committee
                              J. L. Mursell, Member of Committee
                              H. A. Murphy, Major Adviser

Approved by the Committee on the Degree of Doctor of Education
                    Date  *May 10, 1949*

Submitted in Partial Fulfillment of the Requirements for the
Degree of Doctor of Education in the Advanced School of Education

Teachers College, Columbia University
1949

*Copy provided by Special Collections in Music, The University of
Maryland, College Park, Bruce D. Wilson Curator.

The course was interesting to her but proved to be beyond her both intellectually and musically. On the advice of the instructor she dropped the course at the end of the first semester."[25]

On the basis of his study, Leonhard concluded that it was feasible and practical to offer a course in transposition with clefs to mature students, that the skill was a complex one, that a minimum of two semesters would be required to teach it, that the class should be highly selective, and that the students should be highly motivated to learn transposition. He further recommended that only the most intelligent students should be allowed in the course, and that those students should have excellent piano proficiency and thorough music theory training. He thought that many simple tunes in a variety of styles should provide the course material and that many different activities should be used in the course to teach transposition.[26]

On completion of his doctorate, Leonhard remained on the faculty at Teachers College. The College appointed him Assistant Professor of Music Education on July 1, 1950 at an annual salary of $5,000. He remained there for another year, teaching music education and music theory courses.[27]

Lewis B. Hilton, a former student, recalls that Leonhard and Murphy were outstanding teachers in the department at that time. "Both [Leonhard and Murphy] were good musicians and good teachers, but of the two, Charles Leonhard was much the better pedagogue. He was the first and one of very few teachers I have known who was able to

[25]Leonhard, "A Study of the Teaching of Transposition," 22–23.

[26]Ibid., 23.

[27]President of Teachers College, New York, NY, to Charles Leonhard, New York, NY, 8 February 1950, photocopy in possession of the author; and President of Teachers College, New York, NY, to Charles Leonhard, New York, NY, 10 February 1950, photocopy in possession of the author.

put into practice very clearly Deweyan concepts of teaching and imparting knowledge."[28]

Leonhard was able to work with indifferent students needing some "brushup" work in theory. Hilton remembers that "Fortunately one of the brusheruppers was Leonhard. I had expected much humdrum, but he made it extremely lively and absorbing at almost all times."[29] One of the things that made Leonhard's teaching so appealing to students at Teachers College was his propensity to give assignments that students found worthwhile. "Assignments were purposeful and meaningful. I remember many of them 40 years later."[30]

Eunice Boardman, who studied with Leonhard at Teachers College and later at Illinois, recalled that he was especially good in teaching students to create accompaniments to folk and popular songs for school use and analysis at the keyboard. "I was the typical pianist who could play whatever was put in front of me, but in terms of chording and building accompaniments . . . I had figured out how to do it just of out of desperation. So I was terribly impressed with the approach. Even then he had this characteristic about him of being very dynamic, very forceful in his presentation. You were impressed by him."[31]

His work with students at Teachers College, as throughout his career, left a lasting impression and one many remember with gratitude. Hilton said, "I credit Leonhard with a large share of the credit for my becoming a

[28]Hilton to Heller, 3 February 1990.

[29]Ibid.

[30]Ibid.

[31]Eunice L. Boardman, interview by author, 14 October 1990, tape recording and transcript in possession of the author.

respectable theorist and theory teacher at the University level."[32]

Leonhard attributes much of his success in college music teaching to James L. Mursell. Mursell taught several classes Leonhard took, and the two men talked together informally on a regular basis. Mursell gave him an opportunity to speak at a national professional meeting by suggesting that Leonhard take Mursell's place at a session on the teaching of theory at the Music Teachers National Association. Mursell also contributed to Leonhard's development of the concept of comprehensive musicianship. One of the courses that Murphy and Leonhard taught was originally divided into four one-hour classes: harmony, sight-singing, dictation, and keyboard harmony.

> In 1948, Jim observed our classes frequently during an entire semester and wrote a critique of our teaching which I have treasured all of these years. His comments were generally positive, but he ended his critique by asking two questions: "Do you realize how much those four separate hours have in common? Why not merge them?" I took a cue from those questions and merged the content of the four previously separate hours into a course that had the title in the T. C. catalog of "A Unifying Course in Musicianship." I continued to refine my concept of comprehensive musicianship in the theory course I taught at Illinois for 30 years.[33]

As he was completing his dissertation, Leonhard began his scholarly publishing career with a critique of conventional theory teaching and a recommendation for its improvement. He had two publications as a result of a pinch-hitting assignment. Leonhard made an appearance in Chicago during the last week of 1948 and the first week of 1949 at the annual Music Teacher's National Association meeting in place of his mentor, James L. Mursell. The full

[32]Hilton to Heller, 3 February 1990.

[33]Leonhard to Heller, 9 June 1993.

text of his remarks was published in the *Proceedings* of the Association for 1949. A condensed version appeared in the March–April 1949 issue of the *Music Journal*.[34]

His main idea in this paper was to call into question the traditional aims of music theory study which he said were focused around development of skill in four-part harmonization. He called for a re-examination of objectives in teaching theory. It was consistent in style with many iconoclastic statements he would make throughout his career. "We need to . . . concentrate on those values that are worthwhile and durable and have the courage to discard the useless practices no matter how great the break with tradition and convention. Theory must serve a purpose beyond the perpetuation of itself."[35] Strong words from a novice in the profession.

He called the materials used in music theory classes "stilted and unmusical." He said conventional theory submerged creativity, and the courses submitted students to "deadly rigors." He suggested that theory as then taught was "musically so meaningless" because it was based on mechanistic psychology. He lamented the divorce of music and theory and the division between diatonic and chromatic harmony. It was, he said, "ridiculous," and a "deplorable situation." Theory courses were "woefully deficient" in putting their material in a musical context. He noted that harmonization was the main objective "however roundabout or sugar-coated the approach may be." He questioned the powers that be: "Why consider four-part harmonization the Sacred Way?"[36]

---

[34]Charles Leonhard, "A New Approach to Music Theory," *MTNA Proceedings* (1949), 207–214; and Charles Leonhard, "On the Teaching of Theory," *Music Journal* 7 (March–April 1949): 17, 51–52.

[35]Leonhard, "A New Approach to Music Theory," 207.

[36]Ibid., passim.

Traditional approaches to teaching music theory emphasized drill, and they made music conform to the textbook. They made no provision for individualization of instruction, and they used no group dynamics. The sequence was "miserable," and the course was an "utter failure." "The student finishes the course, deposits his notes in the waste-basket on his departure from the class final meeting, with a thankful, 'I'm through with Theory.' . . . His curiosity about music has not been aroused; he has developed little initiative and has no desire or purpose in continuing the study of music structure."[37]

Leonhard was specific about stating his own objectives for theory courses: "1. Ability to understand and manipulate the symbols of music. . . . 2. The ability to read a score, understand it, hear it within one's self, and to interpret it with taste and insight into its meaning. 3. Ability to hear and appreciate the harmonic and structural patterns in compositions. 4. Ability to discriminate between good music and music that is less good. 5. Ability to respond emotionally and intellectually to the inner essence of music (i.e., its tonal and rhythmic patterns)."[38] These, in essence, framed Leonhard's definition of music and what he would later call the aesthetic experience.

Leonhard frankly admitted that he borrowed much of his teaching philosophy from Mursell, specifically, from Mursell's book *Successful Teaching*. In that 1946 publication Mursell had broken the teaching process down into six principles which he labelled focus, context, individualization, socialization, sequence, and evaluation. Leonhard subscribed to Mursell's analysis wholesale.[39]

[37]Leonhard, "A New Approach to Music Theory," 208.

[38]Ibid., 209.

[39]Ibid.; and James L. Mursell, *Successful Teaching: Its Psychological Principles* (New York: McGraw-Hill Book Company, Inc., 1946).

The remainder of the article is a description of how Leonhard taught theory at Teachers College. He listed the materials he used: German chorales, a Beethoven piano sonata (Opus 79, No. 2), Mozart's *Eine Kleine Nachtmusik*, the *Home and Community Song Book* (published by E. C. Schirmer), selected choruses and arias from Handel's *Messiah*, and a sight-singing manual containing folk songs. Students sang frequently in class, and they listened to recordings while reading scores. They wrote short compositions in the styles they were studying. The students took dictation of a regular basis, and they did error-detection exercises.

In sum, Leonhard recommended "The study of the structure of music should be approached through a study of music itself. The learning should be a movement from the essence of music to the externals. The learning should move from synthesis to analysis to synthesis. The emphasis should be on the development of musicianship."[40] He thought his kind of theory course should be placed at the center of all instruction in music. Leonhard closed with a statement urging theory teachers to organize their courses so that the students might learn more effectively. He suggested they become more familiar with developmental psychology in order to do this.

In teaching listening along with performing and creating in his theory classes at Teachers College, Leonhard came to be something of an expert on the availability of recorded musical selections. In 1948, Lilla Belle Pitts arranged a meeting for him with Irving Kolodin. This meeting led to publication of a series of reviews of children's recordings in *The Saturday Review of Literature*. Kolodin (b. 1908) was a New York music critic. In addition to writing regularly in the New York press, he wrote numerous

---

[40]Leonhard, "A New Approach to Music Theory," 214.

books on music. He was one of the first major New York critics to become interested in reviewing music recordings.[41]

Leonhard wrote his reviews of children's recordings in an easy-to-read style for a general audience. He called one recording "First-class nonsense," another "one of those ridiculous stories that send children into gales of laughter and leave adults cold." The reviews credit Leonhard with being an instructor at Teachers College and vice-chair of the Audio-Visual Committee of the Music Educators National Conference.[42]

A year later, Leonhard followed up the *Saturday Review* articles with a piece of advice to elementary teachers in the *NEA Journal*. He addressed classroom teachers' concerns about their lack of musical ability and the availability and cost of equipment and materials. He urged them to begin with relatively easy music that the students could enjoy and sing along with. He urged teachers to pick examples they could respond to physically. He suggested that they teach the children how to operate the equipment and that they play music during recess, at lunch, and before and after school.[43]

Writing to a national audience, Leonhard urged elementary classroom teachers to include music in their study of other subjects, especially geography, history, and literature. To help get the teachers started, he offered a sample lesson and suggested ways they might follow it up later. A footnote identified Leonhard as an assistant

[41]Leonhard to Heller, 1 January 1989; *The New Grove Dictionary of American Music* (1986), s.v. "Kolodin, Irving," by Patrick J. Smith; and Leonhard to Heller, 9 June 1993.

[42]Charles Leonhard, "Records for the Christmas Stocking," *The Saturday Review of Literature* 32 (26 November 1949): 66–67.

[43]Charles Leonhard, "Disc Jockey in the Classroom," *NEA Journal* 39 (November 1950): 588–589.

professor at Teachers College and as national chair of the Recordings Committee of the MENC.[44]

Leonhard completed his trilogy of articles on the use of recorded music with one in the *Music Educators Journal* which he addressed to professionals. It is noteworthy that the first two articles were addressed to general audiences and were totally positive in tone. In writing to professionals, as he had earlier in his MTNA speech, Leonhard again took up a more critical tone. The use of recordings was often "perfunctory and stereotyped." Teachers took records for granted; their use of recordings lacked originality. They were not informed about new releases and used the same examples over and over again. "Our repertoire has ceased to expand."[45]

Leonhard admonished teachers to evaluate recordings for compatibility with course objectives and quality of performance and sound reproduction. Before using the recordings, the teachers should adequately prepare their students. He recognized the power of recorded music to influence students' moods and even their behavior. Furthermore, recordings could provide models, establish musical context, and free the teacher to direct learning activities. Leonhard recommended that teachers demonstrate with their own behavior what they expected of their students while the music was on.

Leonhard counselled the teachers to watch the children closely while the music was playing. Afterwards, he suggested an open discussion about what they heard. "Critical and continuous self-evaluation," he noted, "is our best means of improving our teaching."[46] The article noted that Leonhard chaired the Committee on Records, which was

[44]Leonhard, "Disc Jockey in the Classroom," 588–589.

[45]Charles Leonhard, "On the Use of Recordings." *Music Educators Journal* 37 (February–March 1951): 48–49.

[46]Leonhard, "On the Use of Recordings," 49.

a division of the National Audio-Visual Aids Committee of
the MENC.

In 1949, Leonhard got involved in a project with
Richard G. Kraus, a dance instructor at Teachers College, to
produce a manual for teachers wishing to introduce their
students to square dancing. The result of their work was a
book, *Square Dances of Today and How to Teach and Call
Them*. Kraus wrote the text, Carl Pfeufer furnished the
illustrations, and Leonhard provided the musical
arrangements (i.e., the piano accompaniments). In a preface
to the pianists, Leonhard noted that he wanted to remain true
to the folk character of the dances, while keeping the level of
difficulty within range of amateur accompanists. In all, he
wrote arrangements for thirty-one pieces in the book. In the
preface, Kraus expressed his thanks to his illustrator and "to
Dr. Charles Leonhard, whose excellent arrangements make
the melodies a joy to play—and to dance to."[47]

Mursell had assisted Leonhard with his initial foray
into the music education publications scene. It was not to be
the last time. The New Music Horizons series of Silver
Burdett Company featured two books for junior high school
students entitled *American Music Horizons* (for seventh
graders) and *World Music Horizons* (for eighth graders).
The books' editorial team included Osbourne McConathy,
Russell V. Morgan, Mursell, Marshall Bartholomew, Mabel
E. Bray, Edward Bailey Birge, and W. Otto Miessner. For
the two books, Marion Bauer prepared the listening notes,
Douglas Moore contributed a section on "The Composer at
Work," and Leonhard wrote a unit on reading music.[48]

[47]Richard G. Kraus, *Square Dances of Today and How to Teach and
Call Them,* illustrated by Carl Pfeufer, musical arrangements by Charles
Leonhard (New York: A. S. Barnes and Company, 1950), vii.

[48]Charles Leonhard, "Reading Music," in *American Music Horizons*,
ed. Osbourne McConathy, Russell V. Morgan, James L. Mursell, Marshall
Bartholomew, Mabel E. Bray, Edward Bailey Birge, and W. Otto Miessner
(New York: Silver Burdett Company, 1951), 267–276. See also McConathy
and others, eds., *World Music Horizons*, 251–259.

Figure 13

Piano Accompaniment for "Camptown Races"*

CAMPTOWN RACES

*Kraus, *Square Dances of Today*, 67. © A. S. Barnes and Company, 1950. Used by permission

Leonhard wrote the unit in a casual tone, using first and second person throughout. He began with pitch names, cadences, and phrases. The second section introduces meter signatures, two-four and three-four time signatures, and the half rest. The third portion of the unit presents the major scale and the keys of F and G major. This is followed by basic functional harmony: the tonic and dominant chords. Next come four-four meter, key signatures with two or more flats or sharps, the sub-dominant chord, the bass clef, the dominant-seventh chord, intervals, six-eight meter, minor mode, functional chords in minor modes, and accidentals. A one-page appendix to the unit gives chords for accompaniments in ten major keys.[49]

Working with Silver Burdett on the New Music Horizons series was Leonhard's second adventure with general music classroom series textbooks. It was not to be his last. In the unit he had used numerous examples from folk song literature to demonstrate concepts and to provide children with opportunities to practice the skills associated with them. He would also reprise this strategy in future work.[50]

As he concluded his career at Teachers College, Leonhard took a momentous step in his personal life. He married Ellen Patricia ("Pat") Hagman. Ms. Hagman was an associate professor of health and physical education at Teachers College. She had joined the faculty there in 1945 and was a recognized teacher and scholar at the time she first encountered Leonhard. In 1951, she and the chair of her department, Clifford Lee Brownell, had just completed a

---

[49]Leonhard, "Reading Music," in *American Music Horizons,* 267–276.

[50]Leonhard also had a role in the 1953 revision of the New Music Horizons series. He did some editorial work and wrote some arrangements for the fifth grade book. See Osbourne McConathy, et al., New Music Horizons, fifth book, revised ed. (New York:  Silver Burdett Company, 1953), iii, 202–225.

book with a prophetic title, *Physical Education—
Foundations and Principles.*[51]

In 1951, Leonhard concluded his stay in New York.
Duane Branigan, Director of the School of Music at the
University of Illinois, hired Leonhard to initiate a doctoral
program in music education. Leonhard resigned his position
on the Teachers College faculty, and he and Pat headed west
for a new life in Champaign-Urbana, Illinois. Charles
Walton filled his position at Teachers College.[52]

---

[51] Clifford Lee Brownell and E. Patricia Hagman, *Physical
Education—Foundations and Principles* (New York: McGraw-Hill Book
Company, Inc., 1951); and Barbara L. Bennett, "The Leonhard Connection,"
*Bulletin of the Council for Research in Music Education* 110 (Fall 1991): 19.

[52] *Teachers College Record* 53 (October 1951): 54.

# CHAPTER IV

# THE UNIVERSITY OF ILLINOIS

In the fall of 1951, at the age of thirty-five, Leonhard moved from New York to begin his long career at the University of Illinois. In his new position in Champaign-Urbana, he worked hard to improve the master's and doctoral programs in music education, teach a variety of courses, and supervise doctoral dissertations. All the while, Leonhard maintained an active schedule of participation in professional organizations, research, publications, and public appearances. On the home front, Charles and Pat began their family with the arrival of daughter Alicia in 1952 and son Charles McRae (whom they call Chase) in 1954.

Duane Branigan, Director of the School of Music, hired Leonhard as Associate Professor in Music. On 1 September 1951, the University of Illinois Board of Trustees appointed him to the faculty with the rank of Associate Professor with a salary of $7,500 for the academic year. At that time, only Branigan, John D. Kuypers (Branigan's predecessor as Director of the School of Music), and Mark Hindsley (the Director of Bands) earned higher salaries. Velma Wilson, a veteran Illinois music educator, chaired the music education division.[1]

---

[1]Kritzmire, "The Pedagogy of Charles Leonhard," 113; and University of Illinois, *Transactions of the Board of Trustees, 1950–52,* 1179. Wilson chaired the division until her retirement in 1967. Colleen J. Kirk succeeded her until 1967, when Richard J. Colwell took the position. See Charles Leonhard, Urbana, IL, to George N. Heller, Lawrence, KS, 7 July

Branigan wanted Leonhard to modernize the graduate program and bring it to national prominence. During his first year on campus, Leonhard taught only one course, a seminar in music education. He spent most of his time in that first year making himself known to the music educators in the State of Illinois, researching and preparing the courses he would eventually teach, and planning summer sessions.[2]

The University of Illinois had established a master's degree program in music education in 1939. The nature of that degree was mostly practical and clinical and did not require the students to do very much in the way of original research. The course work emphasized administration, supervision, orchestration, advanced conducting, methods, and clinic work. Just prior to Leonhard's arrival, the University had approved a doctoral program in music education in May of 1951.[3]

The summer session was an important part of Leonhard's plan. In the first two summers (1952 and 1953), visiting faculty included leading general, choral, and instrumental music teachers from public schools in the state and national figures such as Marion Flagg, from Dallas, and Gladys Tipton, then on the faculty at the University of California at Los Angeles. In subsequent years, nationally known music educators who taught in summer sessions at Illinois were Lilla Belle Pitts, Eunice Boardman, Mary Hoffman, June Frazee, Grace Nash, Richard Graham, and Robert Abramson in general music; Weston Noble, Joseph

1993, original in possession of the author; and Colleen J. Kirk, cassette tape response, Tallahassee, FL, 24 March 1990, tape and transcript in possession of the author.

[2]Leonhard to Heller, 1 January 1989; University of Illinois, *Undergraduate Study, 1952–53* (Urbana, IL: University of Illinois, 1952), 401, 838; University of Illinois, *Undergraduate Study, 1954–55* (Urbana, IL: University of Illinois, 1954), 394, 396; University of Illinois, *Graduate Catalog*, 1964–56 (Urbana, IL: University of Illinois, 1964), 208, 210; and Leonhard to Heller, 7 July 1993.

[3]Prince, "Evaluation of Graduate Music Education Programs," 21.

Flummerfelt, and Dorene Rao in choral music; and William
D. Revelli, William Foster, W. Francis McBeth, H. Robert
Reynolds, David Whitwell, Kenneth Bloomquist, and David
Leach in instrumental music.[4]

Leonhard felt that the master's program should serve
the teachers in the schools, to make them better teachers. He
recruited some students into the master's program who may
have been marginally qualified scholastically, but he felt that
their experience in teaching counted for something. He also
felt that they had matured even as scholars in the years that
had transpired since completing their undergraduate degrees.
The doctoral program, however, was highly selective,
admitting fewer than half the applicants.[5]

Soon after arriving at his new position in Champaign-
Urbana, Leonhard began to teach two graduate courses:
Foundations and Principles of Music Education I and II.
These remained staples in the program and led him and one
of his first doctoral students, Robert W. House, to write a
textbook with the same title. For several years, Leonhard's
assignment was the undergraduate course in junior high
school general music, a graduate course in comprehensive
musicianship, and the two foundations courses. In the mid-
nineteen sixties, he gave up the undergraduate course and
thereafter taught the three graduate courses in addition to
supervising doctoral dissertations and conducting a doctoral
seminar.[6]

Clearly, much of the development of graduate courses
was experimental on Leonhard's part. He was using his
experience at Teachers College as a guide to his program at

[4]Leonhard to Heller, 7 July 1993.

[5]Ibid.

[6]Ibid.; Kritzmire, "The Pedagogy of Charles Leonhard," 112;
Bennett, "The Leonhard Connection," 7–9; and University of Illinois
*Undergraduate Study, 1964–65* (Urbana, IL: University of Illinois, 1964),
163. Subsequent issues of the undergraduate catalog show instructors other
than Leonhard teaching the junior high general music course.

Illinois, keeping what worked in his new situation and discarding what did not. Some music theory faculty members may have been concerned about having a music education professor teach a comprehensive musicianship course which could easily be construed as a music theory course. Leonhard tried to set their fears to rest by maintaining that the course was comprehensive and that it was exclusively for music education students who were not likely to take traditional theory courses in any case. During the first few years the course was small, with seven to ten students, all music education majors. In later years, the enrollment rose substantially, and students majoring in other areas of music began enrolling in large numbers.[7]

By 1953, it had become clear that the University needed to hire more faculty in the graduate program in music education. The need was especially acute to have someone with strong research credentials. In 1953, the University hired Bjornar Bergethon to teach and conduct research in music education. Bergethon came to the University in January of 1954 at a higher rank and for a larger salary than Leonhard was earning, and the two men did not get along well. As the years went by, Leonhard became more popular with the students, earned a promotion to the rank of full professor, and surpassed Bergethon in salary. Bergethon retired from the University in 1972.[8]

Leonhard's two-semester sequence in foundations and principles of music education focused on philosophical matters in the first course and psychological topics in the second. He based his work in philosophy on his knowledge

[7]Leonhard to Heller, 7 July 1993.

[8]University of Illinois, *Transactions*, 1952–54 (Urbana, IL: University of Illinois, 1954), 1316, 1534; and Leonhard to Heller, 7 July 1993. Subsequent volumes of the *Transactions* show Leonhard gradually closing on and eventually passing Bergethon in salary. Leonhard was promoted to full professor in 1956, thus eliminating the rank differential. See also, Prince, "An Evaluation of Graduate Music Education," 21.

of and experiences with Susanne K. Langer, James L. Mursell, and others with whom he had studied at Teachers College. He gathered material for the psychological foundations course from his work with Mursell and from his current reading in the field. Among the sources Leonhard used in the second course were such music psychologists as Robert W. Lundin, Carl E. Seashore, Mursell, and Max Schoen. He also drew on the work of learning theorists from the field of psychology.[9]

Leonhard's course in comprehensive musicianship was very much like the theory course he had taught with Howard Murphy at Teachers College. At Illinois, as at Teachers College, he stressed making music theory functional in both listening and performing. A 1987 graduate of the department, Judith Ann Kritzmire, has done an extensive description of Leonhard's teaching of the comprehensive musicianship course. She found that his upbringing, early teaching experiences, and other personal experiences influenced his teaching. Kritzmire concluded that Leonhard tends to regard music as an aesthetic experience and teaching as a psychological and humanistic enterprise.[10]

Doctoral students worked with Leonhard and others in music and in education at the University of Illinois. In 1952, he initiated a doctoral seminar to expose the students to special topics and problems unique to music education and music teacher education. He often brought in guest lecturers from other departments in the University and from other institutions. This also was the forum for doctoral students to present their dissertation proposals and share course

[9]Charles Leonhard, review of *An Objective Psychology of Music*, by Robert W. Lundin, in *Journal of Research in Music Education* 1 (Fall 1953): 141–143; and Bennett, "The Leonhard Connection," 8–9.

[10]Kritzmire, "The Pedagogy of Charles Leonhard," passim; and Bennett, "The Leonhard Connection," 9–11.

syllabuses. The seminar became a required course for students in the doctoral program in 1958.[11]

Robert House and John W. Shepard were the first two Leonhard students to graduate from the program. They finished in 1954. Two more finished in 1955, one in 1956, three in 1957, and four in 1958. Ten of the first dozen students who completed their dissertations in 1954–58 wrote on what might be called descriptive topics. Four of them were program evaluation studies, three were surveys, two were measurement studies, and one was a project to develop instructional materials. Two students wrote what might be called philosophical studies, one on principles for string class instruction and the other on principles for teaching secondary general music.

Many students from the earliest days to the most recent have found Leonhard's personality to be very powerful, almost mesmerizing in its effect on them. House commented that "Basically, I thought of him as a magnetic teacher . . . after a couple of weeks in his class I came under his spell, like a religious conversion. I have been true to that faith ever since . . . ."[12] Dedication pages of the scores of dissertations he supervised and letters from dozens of his students yield similar impressions of Leonhard's ability to affect students in a strong and lasting way.

Students over the years have collected "dicta," or sayings which Leonhard often gave to his classes. They include such gems as "Anadarko, the Pearl of the Washita," "Nobody likes anyone who is perfect, they are a pain," "*Sic transit gloria mundi,*" "If you use imply and infer incorrectly, I'll hit you in the puss," "Life is a game that you

---

[11] Prince, "An Evaluation of Graduate Music Education," 21, 37; and Kritzmire, "The Pedagogy of Charles Leonhard," 11.

[12] Robert W. House, Commerce, TX, to George N. Heller, Lawrence, KS, 23 March 1990, original in possession of the author.

play to the utmost," and "I'm a mechanical moron."[13] These give some insight into the kind of language he used in his classes. The fact that at least one student went to the trouble to collect and distribute copies of them suggests that he tended to leave distinct impressions in students' memories.

Leonhard's supervision of doctoral dissertations is truly monumental. Twelve students finished doctorates under his guidance in 1954–58 and twenty-two students finished in 1959–63. Twenty-three students finished their dissertations and degrees in 1964–68, and thirty-three completed their work in 1969–73. Twenty-seven students finished in 1974–78; thirty-two in 1979–83. Sixteen students graduated in 1984–88, and twelve in 1989–93. All told, Leonhard supervised 177 doctoral dissertations at the University of Illinois from 1951 to 1993, an average of well over four a year. In four of his years at Illinois—1964, 1972, 1973, and 1977—eight of Leonhard's students completed their dissertations. In 1986, he saw ten dissertations to completion, and in 1979 thirteen of his students finished. Eleven of his former students served at least a part of their career on the faculty at Illinois. (See the Appendix for a complete list of Leonhard's doctoral dissertation advisees.)

It is perhaps risky to single out individuals from such a large and distinguished group, but at least three of them are certainly worthy of note: Richard J. Colwell (1961), Bennett Reimer (1963), and Eunice L. Boardman (Meske) (1964). Colwell (b. 1930) came from South Dakota, where he taught in the Sioux Falls public schools. His dissertation topic was "An Investigation of Achievement in Music in the Public Schools of Sioux Falls, South Dakota," and he has since made a reputation in measurement and evaluation of

---

[13]Charles A. McAdams, Warrensburg, MO, to George N. Heller, Lawrence, KS, 3 November 1993, original in possession of the author; and Charles Leonhard, Urbana, IL, to George N. Heller, Lawrence, KS, 1 November 1993, original in possession of the author.

musical achievement and music programs. Colwell joined the faculty at Illinois in 1961 and remained there until 1989. He taught briefly at the University of Northern Colorado in 1989–90 and at Boston University in 1990–1993. In 1993 he joined the faculty at the New England Conservatory in Boston.[14]

Bennett Reimer (b. 1932) came to Illinois from the east coast. He was educated in New York and had taught music and music education at the College of William and Mary and at Madison College, both in Virginia. Reimer was on the music education faculty at Illinois from 1960 to 1965. His dissertation topic was "The Common Dimensions of Aesthetic and Religious Experience." He is well known as a writer on the philosophy of music education, arts in education, secondary general music, and curriculum design. Reimer taught at Case Western Reserve University from 1965 to 1978 and has been the John W. Beattie Professor of Music at Northwestern University since 1978.[15]

Eunice Boardman (b. 1926) grew up in Illinois and Iowa. She took her first degree from Cornell College in Mount Vernon, Iowa, and taught in Iowa public schools while working on a master's degree in music education at Teachers College. It was there she first came in contact with Leonhard. She joined the faculty in music education at Wichita State University in 1955, and while there began doctoral studies at Illinois. Her dissertation was "An Investigation of the Effect of Preschool Training on the Development of Vocal Accuracy in Young Children." Boardman has been influential as an editor of music text book series and as a leader in music teacher education. From 1972 to 1974, she taught at Illinois State University, and in 1975 joined the faculty at The University of

---

[14]*Who's Who in America*, 1990–91, s.v. "Colwell, Richard James."

[15]*The New Grove Dictionary of American Music*, 1986 ed., s.v. "Reimer, Bennett," by George N. Heller.

Wisconsin–Madison. She became director of the School of Music there in 1980. In 1989, Boardman returned to the University of Illinois as a member of the music education faculty. She currently holds the position Leonhard occupied for so many years: Chair of the Committee on Graduate Studies in Music Education.[16]

In addition to teaching, advising, and reading doctoral dissertations, Leonhard engaged in numerous professional activities in the Music Educators National Conference and developed a substantial research and publishing agenda. He continued to serve on the MENC Committee on Recordings in Music Education which he had been on since his days at Teachers College. This was a subcommittee of the MENC Committee on Audio-Visual Aids. Lilla Belle Pitts of Teachers College had headed the Committee from 1948–1951, and Rose Marie Grentzer took over from 1951 through 1955. Richard C. Berg also served on the Audio-Visual Committee during this time and had several articles on the educational uses of television published in the *Music Educators Journal.*[17]

Leonhard also joined the newly formed MENC Committee on Graduate Study in Music Education in 1951. That group was a Sub-Committee of the Committee on Music in Higher Education, of which Earl E. Beach was the chair. Marguerite V. Hood, president of the MENC from 1950–52, had appointed both committees, and they continued to function through the presidency of Ralph E. Rush (1952–54). The Sub-Committee met at the MENC Convention in Philadelphia in 1952 and again in Chicago in 1954 to draft and approve a final report. This committee

---

[16]*Who's Who in America*, 1990–91, s.v. "Boardman, Eunice"; and Boardman interview, 14 October 1990.

[17]"Audio-Visual Aids in Music Education," chap. in *Music in American Education: Music Education Source Book Number Two*, ed. Hazel Nohavec Morgan (Chicago: Music Educators National Conference, 1955), 216–242.

helped lay the groundwork for the content of *Basic Concepts in Music Education*, the 1958 yearbook of the National Society for the Study of Education.[18]

In 1952, A. S. Barnes of New York published Leonhard's first book, *Recreation Through Music*. Mrs. Leonhard had published *Good Health for You and Your Family* for Barnes a year earlier. Leonhard wrote *Recreation Through Music* while in New York. In the preface, he acknowledged his debt to Professor John L. Hutchinson of Teachers College for help in the general field of recreation and to his longtime friend and mentor, Howard A. Murphy.[19]

The 160-page book is a readable compendium of theory and practical advice to persons charged with recreational program management who might want to include music. It defines recreation and lists suitable objectives. It describes the relation of music to recreation and specifies the qualities of a capable leader. In the book, Leonhard discusses listening activities, singing, and instrumental music. The book contains a useful set of references for further study as well as many helpful diagrams and illustrations. A reviewer for the *Peabody Journal of Education* called it an "Excellent guide for the individual who wishes to participate more actively in recreational

---

[18]"Graduate Study in Music Education: A Report of the Committee on Graduate Study in Music Education," *Journal of Research in Music Education* 2 (Fall 1954): 157–170; Leonhard to Heller, 1 January 1989; and Bennett, "The Leonhard Connection," 6–7.

[19]Charles Leonhard, *Recreation Through Music* (New York: A. S. Barnes, 1952), v–vi. Leonhard said in the Preface, "I am most grateful to my wife, Patricia, for her constant encouragement and for her penetrating evaluation of the text from the point of view of the musical amateur." His opening remarks were dated January, 1952, Urbana, Illinois. See also, E. Patricia Hagman, *Good Health for You and Your Family* (New York: A. S. Barnes, 1951). Richard C. Berg, who served with Leonhard on the MENC Audio-Visual Committee, also did a book for A. S. Barnes on marching bands.

music,"[20] and the *Journal of the American Medical Association* even recommended it to doctors who might be interested in occupational therapy.[21]

In 1953, Leonhard brought out his second book, *A Song Approach to Music Reading*. Published by the Silver Burdett Company, this handy volume built on and expanded Leonhard's earlier work for Silver Burdett in the New Music Horizons series. Though the contents of this book obviously came from his own ideas and experiences, he nevertheless inscribed the dedicatory page simply "To Pat."[22]

The procedure would have done Lowell Mason proud. It takes a thoroughgoing rote-to-note approach. The first section, "Exploring Songs with the Ear," has the students learn eighteen folk songs if they did not already know them. In addition to patriotic tunes and hymns the book provides music and words for such standards as "Believe Me, If All Those Endearing Young Charms," "Clementine," and, interestingly, the Sottish folk song, "Charlie Is My Darling."[23]

Part Two of the book begins with a section called "Seeing What You Hear." Here, like a good Pestalozzian music educator, Leonhard presents the symbols for what the students have already experienced: melodic direction and rhythm. Sections in which the students read easy songs, at first with conjunct motion and later with disjunct motion in

[20] "Peabody Bimonthly Booknotes," *Peabody Journal of Education* 30 (September 1952): 120.

[21] "Book Reviews," *Journal of the American Medical Association* 149 (2 August 1952): 1357. See also *The Library Journal*, 15 May 1952, 899.

[22] Charles Leonhard, *A Song Approach to Music Reading*. New York: Silver Burdett Co., 1953. Leonhard wrote a brief article on this topic which appeared in 1952: Charles Leonhard, "A Classroom Teacher and Music Reading," *The Resourceful Teacher* 6 (1952): 12–19.

[23] Leonhard, *A Song Approach to Music Reading*, 3-20.

## Figure 14

### "Charlie Is My Darling," from
### *A Song Approach to Music Reading* (1953)*

READING SONGS

in
*Minor Mode-Various Patterns*
*I and V in Minor*

Sing the refrain of "Charlie Is My Darling" from memory. You will remember that in the discussion of this song in Part One, it was described as a bright gay song. Part of its winsomeness was in the way the singer presented it on the recording, but there was something different about the song itself. When you compared it with "Clementine," another song of sentiment, you probably sensed the great difference in color and mood between the two songs. You are now about to discover what makes the color of these songs so different.

"Clementine" is in *major mode*, while "Charlie Is My Darling" is in *minor mode*. The first phrase of the latter song is notated in Example 82. What key does the signature signify? At first glance you will see nothing unusual about the notation unless you notice that the first skip in the melody is between tones of a chord other than the I chord in E-flat major, the key indicated by the key signature.

Oh, Char - lie  is   my dar - ling, my  dar - ling, my  dar - ling!

Char - lie  is   my  dar - ling, the   young  Che - va - lier!

EXAMPLE 82

·Sing this phrase again, searching with your ear for the key tone. Even though the key signature would seem to indicate that the key tone is E-flat, do you feel like stopping when you get to "young"? When you sing this E-flat have you the sense of repose and relaxation associated with the key tone? No, you do not. There is another "home tone" around which the tones of the E-flat major scale are centered. The new key tone is C(*la*). Try singing the phrase with this key tone in mind and your ear will tell you that this is a fact. This song is in C minor. This is the name of the different pattern created when the tones of the E-flat major scale are regrouped. Because E-flat major and C minor use the same key signature, the key of C minor is said to be the *relative*

*p. 107.  Used by permission of Silver Burdett Ginn, Inc.

chordal patterns. Various meters come into play, and later on the students encounter the bass clef.

Finally Leonhard has the students read more complex songs with skips unrelated to any particular chord, chromatic tones, songs in the minor mode, songs in less common meters, and songs in parts. With the introduction of each new concept, a few short drills follow a short explanation of the concept, and several songs exemplify the concept. Two appendices have helpful scales and chord progressions in major and minor keys and a glossary of common musical terms. All in all, the book is eminently practical and cleverly designed. It drew a nod of approval from Robert E. Nye in a review in the Fall 1953 issue of the *Journal of Research in Music Education.*[24]

Perhaps as a way of advertising his ideas on music reading, and possibly as a way to publicize the book, Leonhard wrote an article on the topic of music reading for the March 1953 issue of the *Music Journal.* In this piece, he presented his ideas on music reading, as carried out in his recent book, at some length. He urged music educators to "reappraise the worth of music reading as an enabling skill and a means to a musical end, and give it intelligent and adequate attention in the music program."[25]

Like the authors of many music reading programs in the mid to late twentieth century, Leonhard followed the language acquisition model, emphasizing listening followed by mastery of symbols. As a careful reader of the works of John Dewey, he urged teachers to organize experiences rather than lecture on music. *"One learns to read music by experiencing and studying music itself and not by arriving at*

[24]Robert E. Nye, review of *A Song Approach to Music Reading,* by Charles Leonhard, in *Journal of Research in Music Education* 1 (Fall 1953): 150–151.

[25]Charles Leonhard, "An Easier Way to Read Music," *Music Journal* 11 (March 1953): 28.

*an intellectual or mathematical understanding of the mysteries of musical notation.*"[26]

While dealing with basic issues in musical literacy, Leonhard was also thinking about curriculum. His work with the MENC Committee on Graduate Study in Music Education and his responsibilities at the University of Illinois no doubt led him to co-author an article on curriculum with a doctoral student, James W. Davidson. The piece described how Leonhard and Davidson worked with the Illinois Secondary-School Principals Association and the Illinois State Department of Public Instruction to write objectives for music in Illinois public schools. Leonhard and Davidson reported the conclusions of the project that music programs need community support, support from other faculty members in the schools, and the understanding and active involvement of school administrators. Furthermore, "The music staff should benefit from directing their teaching toward definite objectives."[27]

Leonhard made a signal contribution to the September 1953 issue of *Education*. Lloyd F. Sunderman, then chair of the music department at the University of Toledo (Ohio) was the special editor for the volume, which was a special issue on the topic of music education. Other authors whose works appeared in the issue were Sunderman, Helen Heffernan, Howard Hanson, Neal E. Glenn, Lillian Baldwin, Theodore F. Normann, Allen P. Britton, and Lilla Belle Pitts. Leonhard's contribution was entitled "Music

[26]Leonhard, "A Easier Way to Read Music," 28, 49. Italics in the original.

[27]James W. Davidson and Charles Leonhard, "The Illinois Curriculum Program and Music Education," *Music Educators Journal* 39 (June–July 1953): 40–42. Davidson was a doctoral student in the College of Education, where he completed his dissertation under Professor Harold C. Hand. Leonhard participated in Davidson's dissertation project and served on his committee. See James W. Davidson, "Construction and Appraisal of Procedures and Materials for Developing Consensus Regarding Music Education Programs" (Ed. D. diss., The University of Illinois, 1954), i, ii, 58, 176.

Education—Aesthetic Education," and in later years he would cite it as the article "which launched the idea of music education as aesthetic education which became the generative idea for the graduate program at Illinois."[28]

Leonhard began his essay with a plea for music educators to emphasize the aesthetic value of music, rather than the instrumental or ancillary values. Mechanistic teaching, undue emphasis on technique, and justification on other than uniquely musical grounds distort the program and lead to the "neglect and abasement of the true and enduring values of music."[29] Teaching music as a means to other ends, such as good health, social development, self-discipline, can lead to emphasis on things that are "transient and spurious when compared with the lasting and authentic values which accrue from experiencing music for its own richly abundant beauty."[30]

Leonhard again wrote on aesthetics in the Spring 1955 issue of the *Journal of Research in Music Education*. The article was originally a speech, one of three given at the March 1954 convention of the MENC in Chicago under the auspices of the Committee on Graduate Study. Leonhard shared the podium on that occasion with E. Thayer Gaston of The University of Kansas and Max Schoen, then of Coe College. Leonhard's talk emphasized the definition of the terms philosophy and aesthetics, and he gave an explanation of philosophical inquiry as a method of research. The article provides a good basis for philosophical research in music education though music educators have tended to ignore this kind of research until fairly recently.[31]

[28]Leonhard to Heller, 1 January 1989.

[29]Charles Leonhard, "Music Education—Aesthetic Education," *Education* 74 (September 1953): 24.

[30]Ibid.

[31]Charles Leonhard, "Research: Philosophy and Esthetics," *Journal of Research in Music Education* 3 (Spring 1955): 23–26.

After a brief survey of the aesthetics of Plato, Immanuel Kant, Hermann von Helmholtz, Wilhelm Wundt, Arthur Schopenhauer, and others, Leonhard recommended the ideas of his teacher, Susanne K. Langer. Because music education students have no systematic training in aesthetics, such as Langer offers, they are forced to use what they know, namely the technical, mechanical, and historical aspects of music and its extrinsic attributes. Attempts to remedy this deficiency should relate philosophy to the students' musical experience, and it should contribute to their practice of the profession. Philosophy, practice, and experience must interact in order to be meaningful.

Two other publications which Leonhard wrote for general educational audiences in the 1950s deserve mention here. Both were reviews of literature in the area of Language Arts and Fine Arts for the American Educational Research Association. One was published in April 1955, the other in April 1958. Both studies briefly summarized the latest books, articles, dissertations, and theses on philosophy and aesthetics, psychology of music, music education history, curriculum, and methods of teaching. Each article concluded with a brief essay on the need for future research. In the 1955 essay, Leonhard reviewed works on sociology of music, and some miscellaneous studies. In the 1958 piece, he reviewed studies of emotion and meaning in music and other miscellaneous studies.[32]

In addition to writing articles and reviewing research for publication, Leonhard also served on the Editorial Committee of the *Journal of Research in Music Education* from 1953 through 1962. In this capacity, he reviewed manuscripts submitted for publication and wrote book reviews for the journal. In the ten years he served on the

---

[32]Charles Leonhard, "Music," *Review of Educational Research* 25 (April 1955): 166–175; and Charles Leonhard, "Music Education," *Review of Educational Research* 28 (April 1958): 159–168.

committee, he seldom attended meetings, which were held at the MENC conventions in even-numbered years.[33]

Many of the books Leonhard reviewed for the *Journal of Research in Music Education* were on topics he was interested in. These included such topics as psychology of music, aesthetics, philosophy of music education, curriculum, teaching methods, and the like. In all, he wrote nine reviews for the *JRME* between 1953 and 1959.[34]

Leonhard's research, reading, and writing about music education and related topics enriched his work on the graduate program at Illinois. At the same time, his experiences with students and faculty informed his research and writing. His contention that philosophy ought to be derived from experience and that it ought to relate to practice had some very practical effects on the graduate curriculum in music education at Illinois during the 1950s. The

[33] Wiley L. Housewright, Tallahassee, FL, to George N. Heller, 27 February 1990, original in possession of the author; and Robert W. John, Athens, GA to George N. Heller, 27 February 1990, original in possession of the author. Britton later recalled that ". . . when Ted [Normann] and I got JRME going, with the absolutely necessary support of Marguerite Hood and Ralph Rush, I asked Charles to serve as a member of the first editorial Committee. He did, and his name appears on the masthead from 1953 through 1962." Allen P. Britton, Ann Arbor, MI, to George N. Heller, 18 January 1989, original in possession of the author.

[34] See Charles Leonhard, review of *An Objective Psychology of Music*, by Robert W. Lundin, in *Journal of Research in Music Education* 1 (Fall 1953): 141–143; Charles Leonhard, review of *Music Education in Action*, by Russell Van Dyke Morgan and Hazel Nohavec Morgan in *Journal of Research in Music Education* 2 (Fall 1954): 188–189; Charles Leonhard, review of *Jean Sibelius*, by Jils-Eric Ringbom, in *Journal of Research in Music Education* 3 (Spring 1955): 66–67; Charles Leonhard, review of *The Enjoyment of Music: An Introduction to Perceptive Listening*, by Joseph Machlis, in *Journal of Research in Music Education* 3 (Fall 1955): 149; Charles Leonhard, review of *Music and Recordings, 1955*, by Frederick V. Grunfield and Quaintance Eaton, in *Journal of Research in Music Education* 4 (Spring 1956): 59–60; Charles Leonhard, review of *Music Education: Principles and Programs*, by James L. Mursell, in *Journal of Research in Music Education* 5 (Spring 1957): 46–47; Charles Leonhard, review of *Writing About Music: A Style Book for Reports and Theses*, by Demar Irvine, in *Journal of Research in Music Education* 5 (Spring 1957): 59; and Charles Leonhard, review of *An Introduction to Music and Art in the Western World*, by Milo Wold and Edmund Cykler, in *Journal of Research in Music Education* 7 (Spring 1959): 151–152.

Department added courses in 1956 on Teaching of Woodwind Instruments and Teaching of Brass Instruments and in 1958 on Advanced Choral Literature and Conducting and Instrumental Clinic and Band Pageantry.[35]

One graduate of the doctoral program from the late 1950s gave credit to Leonhard for helping to develop a stimulating environment for students and for attracting high quality students to it. The students learned many wonderful things from Leonhard, but they also learned much from each other. Leonhard challenged these bright, energetic, and talented people with works from stimulating minds (Dewey, Mursell, Langer, and others), but the students also had "the richness of a great university . . . at our disposal: the concerts, playing in the concert band, the terrific library, etc. Our choice of other faculty was wide and varied."[36]

Leonhard's work in developing courses and his research and writing at Illinois were closely related; his teaching stimulated and guided his research and his research informed and inspired his teaching. Nowhere was this more evident than in his course on foundations and principles of music education. His emphasis on basic principles and his concern with developing philosophical underpinnings for the profession and for his own teaching led him quite naturally from establishing the framework for a graduate program at Illinois to publishing works which would benefit the entire profession.

---

[35]Prince, "An Evaluation of Graduate Music Education," 21.

[36]J. William Worrel, Cincinnati, OH, to George N. Heller, 9 March 1990, original in possession of the author.

# CHAPTER V

# CONCEPTS AND PRINCIPLES

In 1951, Marguerite V. Hood, then president of the Music Educators National Conference, initiated a program under the broad general title of "Music in American Education." Hood appointed numerous committees and subcommittees to study all aspects of music education. Their objectives were (1) to identify new ideas, (2) to involve as many people as possible in bringing these ideas together, (3) to consider music education as a vocation, (4) to identify resources available to music teachers, (5) to consider the needs of exceptional children in music, and (6) to look at music education in a broader context. It was an agenda uniquely tailored to Charles Leonhard's background, training, and interests.[1]

Hood's introduction to the *Music Education Source Book Number Two* of 1955 suggested both a theoretical and a practical concern for music education in the 1950s and beyond. The first chapter set the tone. It was a collection of convention speeches and journal articles addressing the major issue of music's place in the general education of all children. Superintendents of schools, university deans, music supervisors, and music educators of various

---

[1]Marguerite V. Hood, "Music Educators Source Book No. 2," in *Music in American Education: Music Education Source Book Number Two*, ed. Hazel Nohavec Morgan (Chicago: Music Educators National Conference, 1955), viii–ix.

specialties provided material of a philosophical nature which would provide the necessary foundation for the remainder of the book.

The first chapter closed with a brief statement by Leonhard's mentor from Teachers College, Howard A. Murphy, on the duality of music in general education. Murphy defined general education as the effort to prepare youth to deal intelligently with personal and social problems common to all in a democratic society. Music, he said, is important because it clarifies and enriches emotional life, satisfies the need for beauty, and promotes understanding and good will. Music has a duality: aesthetic, universal, and impalpable, serving groups in society on the one hand. Music is also recreational, utilitarian, individual, solitary, and intimate, serving the self. Both perspectives are valid and teachers should stress each one equally when dealing with music as part of a general education program.[2]

The committees on Music in American Education served from 1951 to 1956 under the administrations of MENC presidents Hood (1950–52), Ralph E. Rush (1952–54), and Robert A. Choate (1954–56). During Choate's administration, the Conference launched a second initiative in recognition of the duality in music education of which Murphy had written. Choate appointed a commission on basic concepts to study this problem. He named Thurber H. Madison of Indiana University to chair the committee. The MENC leaders proposed to the National Society for the Study of Education (NSSE) that it publish essays on the philosophical foundations and instructional programs for

---

[2]Howard A. Murphy, "The Duality of Music," in *Music in American Education: Music Education Source Book Number Two*, ed. Hazel Nohavec Morgan (Chicago: Music Educators National Conference, 1955), 17.

music education as a yearbook for the society. The NSSE board approved the project at its February meeting in 1956.[3]

Madison's committee consisted of Oleta Benn of the Carnegie Institute of Technology (Pittsburgh, Pennsylvania), Leonhard, Madison, T. R. McConnell of the University of California, and Theodore F. Normann of the University of Washington. McConnell was a professor of education at California and a member of the National Society for the Study of Education. All the rest were music education professors.

The project was mainly the work of Madison and Leonhard. Allen P. Britton of the University of Michigan had been a member of the original committee, but he resigned from the planning committee when he was asked to become a contributor. "Thurber Madison asked me to join him and Charlie in planning the 'basic concepts' book. Thurber and I had taught together at Charleston, Illinois, in the music department of what is now Eastern Illinois University."[4] Although Madison and Leonhard had been students at Teachers College at different times, they had much in common in their intellectual orientation toward music education. They were united on the idea "that music education as a field of study could profit from a little more intellectuality."[5]

Britton was a long-time friend and peer of Leonhard. He served as founding editor of the *Journal of Research in Music Education* from 1953 to 1972 and was president of the Music Educators National Conference from 1960 to 1962. Like Leonhard, Britton edited a series of books on

[3]Nelson B. Henry, "Editor's Preface," in *Basic Concepts in Music Education*, ed. Nelson B. Henry (Chicago: National Society for the Study of Education, 1958), vii–viii.

[4]Allen P. Britton, Ann Arbor, MI, to George N. Heller, Lawrence, KS, 18 February 1989, original in possession of the author.

[5]Ibid. See also Charles Leonhard, Urbana, IL, to George N. Heller, Lawrence, KS, 4 August 1993, original in possession of the author.

music education for Prentice Hall; Britton's was called the Foundations of Music Education Series. The books were published from 1966 to 1970.[6]

The NSSE Yearbook for 1958, titled *Basic Concepts in Music Education*, provided a much needed intellectual basis for the profession and surveyed topics of interest to practicing music educators as well. It remains an important work on the theoretical aspects of the field. Section One of the book is on disciplinary backgrounds. The section opens with Madison's introductory essay followed by pieces on pragmatism by Foster McMurray of the University of Illinois, realism by Harry S. Broudy also of Illinois, the sociology of music in education by John Mueller of Indiana University, musical experience by George Frederick McKay of the University of Washington, growth processes by James L. Mursell of Teachers College, learning theory by Louis P. Thorpe of the University of Southern California, and the history of music education by Britton.

Section Two of the book was called "Music in the Schools." Clifton A. Burmeister of Northwestern University wrote on "The Role of Music in General Education." Robert W. House wrote on curriculum. William C. Hartshorn, the music supervisor in Los Angeles, wrote on listening. E. Thayer Gaston of The University of Kansas wrote on functional music. Leonhard provided an essay on evaluation, and Oleta Benn wrote the concluding piece, "A Message for New Teachers."[7]

---

[6]*The New Grove Dictionary of American Music*, s.v. "Britton, Allen P.," by Paula Morgan.

[7]Richard J. Colwell has recently edited a sequel to or retrospective of the 1958 NSSE publication, *Basic Concepts in Music Education II* (Niwot, CO: University Press of Colorado, 1991). Colwell's book has reprints of some of the original chapters, rewrites of others by the original authors, and replacements of still others by new authors. Colwell wrote the new chapter on evaluation, replacing the earlier one by his mentor.

Leonhard's essay began with definitions of the terms evaluation and measurement. He then gave eight reasons for evaluation: appraisal of student progress, guidance, motivation, improvement of instruction, improvement of program, student selection, maintenance of standards, and research. Thus the opening strategy was to define and defend evaluation. Once this important task was done, Leonhard set about describing the process. Evaluation begins with objectives, their identification, formulation, and validation. It proceeds with collection and interpretation of data. He discussed the various evaluation tools available to music educators, including tests of musical aptitude and music achievement. In evaluating musical learning, Leonhard urges consideration of musical knowledge, musical understanding, performance skills, listening skills, appreciation, attitudes, and habits. He concluded with a short discussion of the evaluation of music programs.[8]

The book made its appearance in 1958, giving rise to speculation that it was a part of the profession's reaction to the Sputnik crisis of 1957. The truth, however, is that the book was planned many years earlier, as part of the MENC effort to look at music in American education in a general way, and production was well underway before the Russian satellite went into orbit. Nevertheless, the book and Leonhard's contribution to it were invaluable as music educators struggled with ways to respond to criticisms that the American educational system had fallen behind international competition. It helped music educators deal with the many calls for increasing emphasis on academics generally and the sciences in particular as the national interest seemed to dictate.

[8]Charles Leonhard, "Evaluation in Music Education," in *Basic Concepts in Music Education*, ed. Nelson B. Henry (Chicago: National Society for the Study of Education, 1958), 310–338.

In another extremely fortunate case of timing, McGraw-Hill published what many consider the crowning achievement of Leonhard's career, his 1959 collaboration with Robert House, *Foundations and Principles of Music Education.* Many music educators of that time and since have hailed the book's appearance as a much-needed addition to the professional literature, and it has spawned several imitators in subsequent years.

In 1959, House was professor and head of the music department at the University of Minnesota, Duluth. He had been one of Leonhard's first doctoral students at Illinois, completing his degree there in 1954. Like Leonhard, House was an Oklahoman and shared many values with his mentor. Being just five years younger than Leonhard, House made an ideal co-author. House felt that most of the ideas in *Foundations and Principles* came from Leonhard and that his main contribution was to put them in a convincing form for publication. Leonhard had primary responsibility for chapters one, four, five, eight, and eleven, while House drafted chapters two, three, six, seven, nine, and ten using his notes from Leonhard's classes and supplementing them with his own research.[9]

While House may have thought that Leonhard was the source for the book, at least three other important influences can be identified. The first is McGraw-Hill, the publisher. McGraw-Hill had long been engaged in publishing textbooks in the education field. Mursell's 1946 publication, which Leonhard cited in his speech to the Music Teachers National Association was part of a forty-volume series, the McGraw-Hill Series in Education, for which Harold Benjamin was the chief editor.

The second direct inspiration for the book was Leonhard's mentor from Teachers College, James L.

Mursell. Leonhard regarded Mursell as both a superb intellect and a good personal friend. Mursell was adept at organizing ideas and presenting them in written form, a trait that Leonhard admired very much. Mursell was nothing, if not a prolific writer. In his thirty-six year career in higher education, he wrote dozens of books, eight of which pertained directly to music education, and over one hundred articles.[10]

The third source of inspiration for Leonhard and House came from much closer to home: Leonhard's wife, Patricia, had co-authored a similar text for physical education some eight years earlier with Clifford Lee Brownell. The title of the book even foreshadowed Leonhard and House: *Physical Education—Foundations and Principles*. It, too, was published by McGraw-Hill in their Health Education, Physical Education, and Recreation series, of which Brownell was the chief editor. The book's five sections, on motivation, program, instruction and supervision, administration, and evaluation, show some similarities to Leonhard and House, though it cannot be said that the later work follows the earlier one very closely in either form or content.[11]

---

[10]For complete lists of Mursell's works, see Simutis, "James Lockhart Mursell"; Metz, "The Philosophy and Psychology of James Mursell"; and O'Keefe, "James Lockhart Mursell." In addition to *Successful Teaching* (1946), Leonhard and House cited the following Mursell works in the first edition of *Foundations and Principles*: *The Psychology of Music* (New York: W. W. Norton & Company, Inc., 1937); *Education for Musical Growth* (Boston: Ginn & Company, 1948); *Principles of Democratic Education* (New York: W. W. Norton & Company, Inc., 1955); *Music Education Principles and Programs* (Morristown, NJ: Silver Burdett Company, 1956); and Mursell's chapter, "Growth Processes in Music Education," in *Basic Concepts in Music Education*, ed. Nelson B. Henry, (Chicago: National Society for the Study of Education, 1958), 140–162.

[11]Clifford Lee Brownell and E. Patricia Hagman, *Physical Education—Foundations and Principles* (New York: McGraw-Hill Book Company, Inc., 1951). Mrs. Leonhard also co-authored two other books on teaching physical education: Clyde Guy Knapp and E. Patricia Hagman, *Teaching Methods for Physical Education: A Textbook for Secondary*

The preface to the first edition of *Foundations and Principles* identifies historical, philosophical, and psychological matters as the foundations of music education. The principles are concerned with program development, methods of teaching, administration, supervision, and evaluation. This conceptualization of the topic recalls Howard Murphy's idea of the duality music teaching and the structure of *Basic Concepts*. This was the scheme of the two courses Leonhard had developed for the graduate program at Illinois, also called Foundations and Principles of Music Education.

In addition to Mursell, the foundations part of the book leans heavily on the work of John Dewey, Susanne K. Langer, Max Schoen, Carl E. Seashore, and Leonard B. Meyer. To a lesser extent, Leonhard and House refer to the work of music educators and psychologists Paul R. Farnsworth, E. Thayer Gaston, Kate Hevner (Mueller), Jacob Kwalwasser, Robert W. Lundin, and Lowell Mason.

The first chapter, "The Objectives and Processes of Education," lays the groundwork for the whole. In it, Leonhard and House argue that "the primary purpose of the music education program is to develop the aesthetic potential, with which every human being is endowed, to the highest possible level."[12] They urge music educators to develop a program that would make a unique contribution to education, to develop a sound philosophy of music education, and to make clear statements of goals and objectives. The authors urged school music teachers to attend carefully to the processes of curriculum, instruction, administration, supervision, and evaluation.

*School Teachers* (New York: McGraw-Hill, 1953); and Clyde Guy Knapp and Patricia Hagman Leonhard, *Teaching Physical Education in Secondary Schools* (New York: McGraw-Hill, 1968).

[12]Leonhard and House, *Foundations and Principles*, 1.

Chapter Two, "The Role of Principles in Music Education," makes the case that music educators should investigate, formulate, and apply specific principles in the course of their work. For Leonhard and House, principles are fundamental truths which help a person decide how to act. "They are derived from all pertinent information concerning [a person's] biological and sociological inheritance."[13] Despite their law-like qualities, principles are constantly in need of revision as newer and better information becomes available, and will necessarily vary from one individual and one situation to another.

"The Historical Foundations of Music Education" (Chapter Three) affirms the status of music as an element of culture and the long-standing need for effective methods of music education. Schools have included music in their course of study from the earliest times of Western civilization, and American colonists established singing-schools from the outset of their very first settlements in the New World. Music has been an important part of basic education in American schools ever since.

Leonhard and House draw heavily from John Dewey and Susanne Langer in Chapter Four on "Philosophical Foundations of Music Education." They begin by defining the very term, philosophy, and defending the need for a philosophy of music education. They stress Dewey's idea of art as experience as a foundation for building a philosophy of music education, and they define aesthetic experience in accordance with the ideas of Dewey, Langer, and Max Schoen. Responses to music, they say, may be musical or unmusical, technical or critical; and human beings make value judgments about music as a consequence of their experience with it. Music has been included in the school curriculum for a variety of reasons, not all of them justifiable.

[13]Leonhard and House, *Foundations and Principles*, 37.

In "The Foundations of Musical Learning" (Chapter Five), Leonhard and House adopt Mursell's definition of learning as the basis for their work. Mursell stressed the importance of meaning in learning, thus, "Music education is properly concerned with the explication of musical meaning."[14] The authors proceed to discuss meaning in music. They note the contribution of Leonard B. Meyer in establishing absolutist and referential constructs of musical meaning. Meyer's analysis leads to identification of embodied and associative meanings. If music education is essentially aesthetic education, then it became important for Leonhard and House to treat the role of perception in musical learning. This led naturally to an examination of the products of musical learning: appreciation, understanding, knowledge, skills, attitudes, and habits. After a discussion on maturation and music learning, the chapter concludes with a survey of learning theories and principles.

Leonhard and House discuss the "Objectives for Music Education" in Chapter Six. They first deal with the function of objectives in music education and then give some guidance to music educators in formulating objectives. Their principles for writing objectives take into account the aims of a democratic society, social circumstances, social change, human needs, and the need to develop individual capacity. In addition, objectives should be compatible with one another, they should be attainable, and they should be readily applicable to the program. The authors end the chapter with statements of objectives for classes in general music, performance (band, choir, and orchestra), theory and composition, and musicology.

Chapter Seven, "The Music-Education Program," reflects some of the thinking in House's article, in *Basic Concepts*. It speaks of the substance of the music program

---

[14]Leonhard and House, *Foundations and Principles*, 138.

and determining the experiences to be included in it. It has notes on organizing and implementing the program. The text identifies guiding principles which help music educators conceive their programs in terms of individual experiences and determine them on the basis of objectives. It encourages program development in terms of the most favorable means of student learning and basing programs on continuing evaluation. The chapter recommends involving everyone in program development, letting the program evolve gradually, having an orderly sequence, and dividing the program into a series of related forms of activity. Leonhard and House suggest that music educators allow for unique and individual patterns of experience, and outline each segment of the program in terms of practical elements of daily instruction. The chapter closes with a discussion of the operational levels of the music program in elementary schools, secondary schools, and higher education.

"Methods of Teaching Music" is the subject of Chapter Eight. Once again, the authors begin with a definition, this time of teaching and teaching methods. They categorize the different types of methods as teacher centered and student centered. They define success in terms of student achievement. Music methods, say Leonhard and House, are based on the subject matter, objectives, and the learning process. Teachers must take into account their students' maturational levels, experiential backgrounds, and present needs. Teaching also depends upon teacher competencies and logistical matters, such as material, equipment, facilities, time available, and class size. The authors give clear and concise hints for teaching performance skills, music reading, appreciation, knowledge, understanding, and attitudes. Their principles of music teaching include establishing objectives, selecting subject matter and experiences likely to lead to the desired behavior, and providing for the active participation of the students. They recommend that teachers use several different kinds of media, arrange sequences to move from concrete to abstract, and motivate students strongly. Leonhard and House also urge teachers to individualize instruction whenever possible, provide opportunities for exploratory experiences, emphasize creativity in all music instruction, and establish a favorable social climate in the classroom.

In Chapter Nine, "Administration of the Music Program," Leonhard and House summarize administrative patterns and talk about types of administration (autocratic, laissez-faire, and democratic). They describe the administrative process and characteristics of administrators. Their principles of administration include definitions of responsibility, authority, and policy. They note that "Administrative procedure should be adapted to the changing needs of the situation."[15] The authors divide the tasks into program administration, personnel administration, and administration of materials, equipment and facilities. They conclude the chapter with a discussion of relations between teachers and administrators.

Leonhard and House consider the topic of "Supervision in Music Education" (Chapter Ten) by examining the conduct, function, and process of music supervision. They describe the attributes of competent music supervisors and the work of supervision. Their principles of supervision include planning and adherence to program objectives and continual evaluation. They note that supervision should promote creative and objective methods of improving instruction and seek to develop students and teachers. "Music supervision should be conducted

---

[15]Leonhard and House, *Foundations and Principles*, 281.

informally and flexibly [and] should move gradually to produce a united effort for more effective instruction."[16]

Chapter Eleven, "Evaluation in Music Education," brings the book to a close. It follows Leonhard's chapter of the same title in *Basic Concepts* very closely. This chapter defines the term and describes its uses (appraisal of pupil progress, guidance, motivation, improvement of instruction, maintenance of standards, and research). It defines and explains relevance, validity, reliability, and other factors in selecting evaluation tools and gives some procedures for selecting evaluation instruments. This chapter has much useful information on evaluating students, evaluating the music program, and the preparation and validation of objectives.

The reviews of the book were mixed. An unsigned review in *The Instrumentalist* called it a "welcome addition to the college texts on music education."[17] On the other hand, writing in the *Music Educators Journal* and the *Journal for Research in Music Education*, Leonhard's colleague from the MENC Sub-Committee on Graduate Studies and the Commission on Basic Concepts, Theodore F. Normann, was a little more critical. Noting numerous predecessors to this kind of volume, Normann wrote that "One finds very little in this study that can be called radically new or different. . . . They point no finger to the future nor do they examine with a firm and discerning eye those features of music which characterize most clearly our American

---

[16]Leonhard and House, *Foundations and Principles*, 313.

[17]Review of *Foundations and Principles of Music Education*, by Charles Leonhard and Robert W. House, in *The Instrumentalist* 14 (February 1960): 6.

culture." Normann did, however, give the book his approval, despite these criticisms.[18]

Most critics in the music education profession warmly endorsed the book, and professors across the country made it a standard text in the field for over a decade. The book attracted so much interest and got so much use in the 1960s, that McGraw-Hill asked Leonhard and House to bring out a revised edition. This they did in 1972. House, by then was director of the School of Music at Southern Illinois University, Carbondale.

In the preface to the second edition, the authors noted the enthusiastic reception the book had received. The revisions in the new edition reflected recent developments in music and music education, and well as in the related fields of aesthetics, education, and psychology. The general organization, however, remained basically the same.[19]

The third chapter on historical foundations contains a new paragraph on Kodály and brief discussion of electronic music, Suzuki, the cultural explosion of the 1960s, research in music education, and the Contemporary Music Project. Leonhard and House also revised the questions for further study and expanded the list of references at the end of the chapter.

In the second edition, the fourth chapter, which takes up the philosophical foundations of music education, adds a discussion of the so-called new musics: ethnic and contemporary. It also considers questions pertaining to youth music (a hot topic in music education in the late 1960s and early 1970s) and experimental music: "Youth music and

[18]Theodore F. Normann, review of *Foundations and Principles of Music Education*, by Charles Leonhard and Robert W. House, in *Music Educators Journal* 46 (February–March 1960): 110; and *Journal of Research in Music Education* 8 (Spring 1960): 51–53.

[19]Charles Leonhard and Robert W. House, *Foundations and Principles of Music Education*, 2nd ed. (New York: McGraw-Hill Book Company, 1972), viii.

experimental music have become potent forces in the musical life of the world and cannot be ignored in the construction of a philosophical orientation for music education."[20]  This chapter, too, has revised questions for further study and more references at the end of the chapter.

The new Chapter Five, "Foundations of Musical Learning," expands on the contributions of learning theorist B. F. Skinner and introduces new material on Jean Piaget, David P. Ausubel, and Robert Gagné. The authors give new suggestions for further research in a section on "A Program for the Future."  In response to recent developments in psychology, Leonhard and House advise music educators that "A more fruitful alternative to past practice may lie in subjecting musical learning to searching analysis to determine what different types of learning are involved in musical learning as a whole."[21]  As with previous chapters, the authors changed the study questions and reference list to accommodate new material.

The revised sixth chapter on objectives substitutes the word initiatives for habits.  The first edition had objectives classified according to how they pertained to knowledge, understanding, skills, attitudes, appreciations, and habits. The second edition retains the first five classifications, but changes the sixth one from habits to initiatives.  The text discussing this last category remained virtually the same as in the first edition.  In a lengthy section, the new edition recommends the objectives of the National Assessment of Educational Progress for use in general music classes.[22]

[20]Leonhard and House, *Foundations and Principles*, 2nd ed., 109.

[21]Ibid., 168.

[22]Eleanor L. Morris and John E. Bowes, eds., *Music Objectives* (Denver, CO: National Assessment of Educational Progress, Education Commission of the States, 1970). For a thorough discussion of the NAEP, see Michael L. Mark, *Contemporary Music Education*, 2nd ed. (New York: Schirmer Books, 1986), 335–354.

The most extensively revised chapter was Chapter Seven, "The Music Education Program." Leonhard and House expanded most sections in the new edition. They added material on Orff-Schulwerk, core curriculum, meeting local needs, outlining instruction, and secondary general music. They also updated the reference list at the end of the chapter and added new state curriculum guides.

In a brief section on music teacher education appearing in the second edition, Leonhard and House seem to approve of the music education curriculum recommended by the National Association of Schools of Music. This is an interesting position, in light of the study then being undertaken by the Music Educators National Conference under the leadership of Robert H. Klotman and in light of the activities Leonhard would engage in to organize music teacher education in the 1980s.[23]

The remaining chapters in the second edition had little or no revision. Chapter One on "The Objectives and Processes of Education," and Chapter Ten on supervision, had no changes at all. Chapters Two, on "The Role of Principles in Music Education," Eight on methods, Nine on administration, and Eleven on evaluation had mostly minor revisions and updates of questions and references.

The new edition impressed reviewers much more than the original. Perhaps Leonhard and House were more forward looking than Theodore Normann and others of the late fifties were willing to admit. Katherine Crews in the *Music Educators Journal* expressed the hope that readers of

[23]See Harold F. Abeles, Charles R. Hoffer, and Robert H. Klotman, "Teacher Education and Future Directions," chap. in *Foundations of Music Education* (New York: Schirmer Books, 1984), 321–338. This book was one of two that came out in 1984 seeking to replace Leonhard and House, *Foundations and Principles of Music Education* as a basic text for graduate study in music education. The other was Malcolm Tait and Paul A. Haack, *Principles and Processes of Music Education: New Perspectives* (New York: Teachers College Press, 1984). The first words of each title give clues as to their model.

the book would use it as a guide and inspiration to formulating a sound philosophy and so improve their teaching. The material in Leonhard and House, she said, provided what was needed.[24]

Paul R. Lehman, writing in the *Journal of Research in Music Education*, called the new edition "*au courant,* . . . their currency is a tribute to the farsightedness of the authors." He called the book and its predecessor "the preeminent textbook for courses in the foundations of music education. The second edition, still authoritative and thorough, has reasserted and justified that claim to dominance. No music education student should be unacquainted with it."[25]

A brief, unsigned review in *The American Music Teacher* (the official journal of the Music Teachers National Association) called the first edition influential in music education throughout the world. Commenting on the second edition, the reviewer wrote that "Undergraduates and graduates will find this book helpful as a basic text for music teacher preparation programs."[26]

Leonhard's contributions to the professional literature had great impact. Music educators looked to him and to his peers in higher education for leadership as the cold war heated up and domestic problems gave rise to increasing concerns about the American educational system and music's place in that system. As the Eisenhower administrations of the 1950s gave way to the Kennedy-Johnson years of the 1960s, people began to believe that concerted action by the

[24]E. Katherine Crews, Review of *Foundations and Principles of Music Education*, by Charles Leonhard and Robert W. House, 2nd ed., in *Music Educators Journal* 59 (March 1973): 82–86.

[25]Paul R. Lehman, Review of *Foundations and Principles of Music Education*, 2nd ed., by Charles Leonhard and Robert W. House, in *Journal of Research in Music Education* 21 (Summer 1973): 190–191.

[26]Review of *Foundations and Principles of Music Education*, by Charles Leonhard and Robert W. House, 2nd ed., in *The American Music Teacher* 22 (November–December 1972): 43.

government and other institutions in the society could resolve whatever problems the nation might have.

In 1961, the Office of the Superintendent of Public Instruction of the State of Illinois issued a bulletin on *Learning and Living Music*. E. Arthur Hill, director of music education for the public schools of Elgin, Illinois, chaired the project, and Leonhard served on both the advisory and editorial committees. The bulletin presents the case for a well-balanced program in music which emphasizes musical experience. It gives teachers a brief rationale for and defense of music in the school curriculum, and then sets forth guidelines for music in pre-school, primary and intermediate grades, and middle-level schools. It also has sections on instrumental and choral music ensembles and organizations. This publication reflects Leonhard's ideas in its call for careful planning, attention to aesthetic values, and systematic evaluation.[27]

In the early 1960s, Leonhard began to speak more and more frequently to music educators as they met in their state associations. This was a kind of grass roots approach, and he started it in his native state of Oklahoma. Speaking before the Oklahoma Music Educators Association in 1961, Leonhard challenged members of his audience to create a coordinated music education program that extended across all twelve years of public schooling. He felt that while music teachers were better prepared than ever, the number of music specialists in the schools was inadequate to meet the students' needs. Music educators, he said, must avoid over-specialization and compartmentalization in themselves and in their programs.[28]

---

[27]*Learning and Living Music* (Springfield, IL: Office of the Superintendent of Public Instruction, 1961).

[28]Charles Leonhard, "A Challenge to Music Educators: A Twelve-Year Coordinated Music Program," *Oklahoma School Music News* 12 (December 1961): 3–7.

Figure 15

Leonhard Speaking to the Oklahoma
Music Educators Association, 1961*

*Oklahoma School Music News* 12 (December 1961): 3. Used by
permission. Photograph provided by Special Collections in Music, The
University of Maryland, College Park, Bruce D. Wilson, Curator.

Even where specialization and compartmentalization could not be avoided, music educators should work to coordinate them for greatest efficiency and effectiveness. Leonhard also noted an imbalance of emphasis on performance objectives over the needs of students' general musicianship, and he criticized programs that lacked sequence and continuity "The challenge of our mission is to reveal to all our people the timeless meanings in music, to introduce them through musical experience to the realm of the aesthetic in which life gains some of its most enduring and worthwhile values, and to educate them so that they can bring to their lives the full inspiring force of the beauty and grandeur of the musical message."[29]

In addition to speaking before state meetings of music educators, Leonhard continued to work with his peers in higher education. The University of Illinois was one of the major universities of the Midwest, known collectively as the Big Ten. The universities in this group with strong music schools and departments have exerted major leadership in music education over the years, and the 1960s were no exception. In 1962, Big Ten schools with music teacher education programs joined to form a music education section of the Council for Institutional Cooperation (CIC). Faculty members and doctoral students from participating institutions have met annually since then. Leonhard was an active participant in these sessions from 1962 until 1986.[30]

One of the hundreds of meetings held by educational leaders in the 1960s occurred in Columbus, Ohio under the auspices of the School of Music, the College of Education, and the Graduate School of The Ohio State University. The meeting was called Current Issues in Music Education—A Symposium for College Teachers of Music Education.

[29]Leonhard, "A Challenge to Music Educators," 7.

[30]Leonhard to Heller, 4 August 1993.

Leaders in music education from around the Midwest met on the campus in Columbus on February 15–16, 1963. They took up three main topics at the meeting: learning theory, laboratory experiences, and the role of the arts in education. Leonhard gave the opening presentation on learning theory.[31]

Leonhard's presentation opened with a tribute to Carl E. Seashore and James L. Mursell for their work earlier in the century and criticized music educators of the 1960s for failing to follow up on their ideas. He then surveyed general educational psychologists, beginning with Edward L. Thorndike, Skinner, Piaget, and Ausubel. Leonhard had hinted at some of this material in Chapter Five of the first edition of *Foundations and Principles*, and much of what he spoke on in Columbus in 1963 found its way into the second edition. He concluded his talk with a plea for more experimental research in the application of learning theory to practical problems in music education. He recommended restructuring graduate programs to allow students to specialize in this area, and he urged colleges and universities to create research positions on their faculties.[32]

[31]George H. Wilson, ed., *Current Issues in Music Education—A Symposium for College Teachers on Music Education* (Columbus, OH: The Ohio State University, 1963), i–vi.

[32]Charles Leonhard, "Newer Concepts in Learning Theory as They Apply to Music Education," in *Current Issues in Music Education—A Symposium for College Teachers of Music Education*, ed. George H. Wilson (Columbus, OH: The Ohio State University, 1963), 1–9. Essentially the same text is in *Council for Research in Music Education Bulletin* 1 (June 1963): 24–31; and in Leonhard's chapter, "Learning Theory and Music Teaching," in *Comprehensive Musicianship: The Foundation for College Education in Music* (Washington, DC: Music Educators National Conference, 1965), 49–58. Carl E. Seashore (1866-1949) took a Ph.D. in psychology from Yale in 1895, He taught at the University of Iowa from 1902 until his death. His life-long interest in music led him to pioneering research and writing on such matters as the measurement of aural perception, graphic representation of musical performance, vibrato, and aesthetics. People remember Seashore today for his *Measures of Musical Talent* (1919), a test of discrete aural skills. See *The New Grove Dictionary of American Music* (1986), s.v. "Seashore, Carl E.," by Ramona H. Matthews.

In 1963, Leonhard and Richard J. Colwell, began the *Bulletin of the Council for Research in Music Education.* The first issue came out in June of 1963 and included a reprint of Leonhard's Ohio State University address on learning theory. Colwell edited the *Bulletin* for twenty-six years, assisted by an advisory committee and the Council. Leonhard served on the initial advisory committee with Colleen J. Kirk of the University of Illinois and William L. Johnston, of the Office of the Illinois Superintendent of Public Instruction. Leonhard also served as a member of the Council from its inception in 1963 until the fall of 1987.[33]

Leonhard was not only active in presenting his ideas to state associations and peers in music in higher education. In 1963 he addressed a much wider audience in writing on the place of music in elementary and secondary education for the *NEA Journal*, expressing a philosophical position to the education world at large. He made a pitch for the study of music as a significant human achievement, a unique symbol system, and a valuable aesthetic experience. He cautioned against turning music education into a recreational program or a means for emotional catharsis. Music instruction must be aimed at "its logical role in education for richer living . . . the purpose of the music program is to develop musical competence, musical understanding, and knowledge of the whole range of music literature in all students."[34]

All was not quiet on the home front during these years. One may get the impression from all Leonhard's publications and public speaking during these years that he was hardly ever at his post in Champaign-Urbana. The record shows

[33]Richard J. Colwell, Greeley, CO, to George N. Heller, Lawrence, KS, 11 February 1990, original in possession of the author. Johnston was one of Leonhard's students. His dissertation was "An Appraisal of Music Programs in the Public Schools of Illinois Excluding Chicago" (Ed.D. diss., The University of Illinois, 1966).

[34]Charles Leonhard, "The Place of Music in Our Elementary and Secondary Schools," *NEA Journal* 52 (April 1963): 40–42.

otherwise. He taught his courses, constantly refining them and developing them in light of new information and research, and he contributed significantly to growing knowledge of the field, both in his own research and in that of his students which he supervised. In the years from 1958 to 1964, thirty-two students completed doctoral dissertations under his supervision. Topics included development of instructional materials, philosophical investigation, tests and measurements, program evaluations, historical studies, bibliographical research, and status studies. (See Appendix.)

Leonhard worked diligently in developing his ideas about music education and presenting them to his students and to the wider public in and outside the profession. He taught a full load of classes and supervised a large number of doctoral dissertation projects. As the Sputnik crisis faded, other concerns rose to the surface. The struggle for civil rights increased throughout the 1960s culminating in the riots late in the decade, and student opposition to the increasingly violent war in Southeast Asia caused educators in all fields to reconsider their fundamental beliefs and values. Leonhard was out in front on much of this, and thus he was in a unique position to deal with the interaction of theory and practice, of philosophies and programs. His ideas about aesthetic education were not simply pie-in-the-sky formulations of a curious intellect; his practical suggestions for day-in-day-out music teaching were not limited to his own experience. His approach grounded theory in practice and used philosophy to guide and direct programs.

# CHAPTER VI

# AESTHETIC EDUCATION
# IN THEORY AND PRACTICE

The American people experienced the extremes of both hope and frustration in the years from 1965 to 1974. Lyndon B. Johnson, Vietnam, Civil Rights, Watergate, the Great Society, Martin Luther King, Robert F. Kennedy, and Richard M. Nixon symbolize a few of the currents swirling about the nation in those tumultuous years. In less obvious ways xerography, cassette recordings, and heart transplants were changing life in the United States and around the world. So too were the Elementary and Secondary Education Act, the National Foundation on the Arts and Humanities, the International Education Act, the Educational Professions Development Act, and the Public Broadcasting Act.

Music education experienced the Tanglewood Symposium in 1967. Karl D. Ernst and Charles L. Gary published *Music in General Education* in 1965 and the MENC put out its *Source Book III* in 1966. The *MMCP Synthesis* appeared in 1965. Silver Burdett had brought out its new series, Making Music Your Own in 1964, and Holt Rinehart and Winston entered the lists with Exploring Music in 1966. Ginn also had a new series in 1966, The Magic of Music, as did the Follett Publishing Company.

In the late 1960s and early 1970s, Charles Leonhard was very much concerned with philosophical matters, particularly teleology and aesthetics. The two great questions that appear in his writings from this period were: What are the proper aims and ends of music education, and what constitutes the proper means for attaining them? He framed the goals and objectives question by thinking and writing about what might transpire in music and music education over the next ten years. He also considered the question of means to be critical to his ideas about aesthetic education.

The Seminar on Comprehensive Musicianship was an epoch-making meeting. It met at Northwestern University in Evanston, Illinois, on April 22–25, 1965. For four days, leaders in music education theory and practice met and discussed new ways to approach the training of music teachers in American colleges and Universities. Five "distinguished experts" provided background papers for the conference: James C. Carlsen, then at the University of Connecticut; Allen Forte of Yale University; William Mitchell of Columbia University; Ole Sand, then director of the Center for the Study of Instruction of the National Education Association; and Leonhard. Leonhard found that the Seminar "was unique in my experience in that music educators, theorists, composers, musicologists, and psychologists joined in serious extended consideration of the question of how best to develop musicianship. It was without doubt the most exhilarating four days I ever spent in a professional meeting."[1]

Leonhard's presentation to the seminar was on the philosophy of music education. In it he took the position that philosophical deliberation was eminently practical. He called philosophy a basic system of beliefs, rather than an approach to knowledge. These beliefs, he wrote, provided music educators with a foundation for their teaching and

[1]Charles Leonhard, Urbana, Il, to George N. Heller, Lawrence, KS, 25 August 1993, original in possession of the author.

could help explain the endeavor to both those within it and those outside. While this definition may be more akin to ideology than to philosophy, it was typical of academic thinking in the 1960s and remains much in vogue in the 1990s.[2]

Leonhard defined music education as "all deliberate efforts to educate people in music regardless of level or area of specialization."[3] Defining music education as efforts to educate people in music is obviously tautological, but the intent was to expand the idea beyond schooling "to include every aspect of music teaching and learning regardless of level . . . or focus . . . ."[4] He sought to have the term "music education" stand for more than just "public school music."

The prevailing philosophy of music education in the mid-1960s, Leonhard said, was a form of instrumentalism, That is music should be taught because it enhanced the non-musical or extra-musical development of children. Music contributed to good health, proper behavior, industriousness, and so forth. Despite the success of this approach, Leonhard put forward the ideas of Harry S. Broudy on realism and Foster McMurray on pragmatism—both taken from the 1958 publication of *Basic Concepts in Music Education*.[5]

[2]Charles Leonhard, "The Philosophy of Music Education—Present and Future," in *Comprehensive Musicianship: The Foundation for College Education in Music* (Washington, DC: Music Educators National Conference, 1965), 42–49. This same text appeared as "Philosophy of Music Education," *Music Educators Journal* 52 (September–October 1965): 58–61, 177. Leonhard also presented a paper to the Northwestern seminar on "Learning Theory and Music Teaching." It was published in *Comprehensive Musicianship*, 49–58, and had also been published earlier.

[3]Leonhard, The Philosophy of Music Education—Present and Future" (CMP), 42.

[4]Leonhard to Heller, 25 August 1993.

[5]Leonhard, "Philosophy of Music Education" (*MEJ*), 58–61.

Music educators run certain risks in appealing to outsiders for their philosophical foundations, however. The dangers are twofold: people from other fields are not as intimately aware of the problems and prospects of the field, and their formulations are not always clearly understood by music educators. The solution for this was to have undergraduate and graduate students in music education study aesthetics, to create graduate specialties in aesthetics, to endow professorial chairs in the philosophy of music education, and to hold symposia on the philosophy of music education involving music educators and scholars from related disciplines.[6]

Leonhard was a member of Group II of the Seminar, which the Seminar organizers charged with making recommendations on musical analysis and aural skills. William Thompson, chairman of the Theory Department at Indiana University chaired the group. In a final report, the members of Group II recommended that materials used in aural training be drawn from various historical periods and cultures and that teachers utilize the latest findings in educational psychology. They also recommended that music educators place more emphasis on individualized instruction and do more singing and playing of instruments. The group further suggested that music educators relate music theory to other music performing activities more. Analysis should result in students as listeners who could organize and comprehend what they hear. Students as performers should be aware of the structure of music. As composers, students should understand historical styles.[7]

[6]Leonhard, "The Philosophy of Music Education—Present and Future" (CMP), 48.

[7]Group II of the Northwestern Seminar consisted of Leslie Bassett, The University of Michigan; Robert Cogan, New England Conservatory of Music; Allen Forte, Yale University; Thomas Gorton, The University of Kansas; Paul Harder, Michigan State University; Helen M. Hosmer, Crane Department of Music, State University College, Potsdam, New York; James Paul Kennedy, Bowling Green State University; Beth Landis, Riverside,

Leonhard was involved in much more than simply theorizing about music education. In 1965, he became involved in a project for the Georgia Educational Television Network, entitled, "Pathways to Discovering Music." Leonhard worked with the Georgia State Department Television Network to produce tapes which could help inservice elementary classroom teachers do a better job teaching music. The project culminated in a series of four television tapes. Frank Crockett, Music Consultant in the Georgia State Department of Education and a former Leonhard doctoral student, commented that "His approach is not exactly the usual one, and is fully as valuable and interesting to the special music teacher as to the classroom teacher."[8] The phrase, Discovering Music, was significant to Leonhard and would find its way into the title of a related project very soon after the completion of the Georgia television series.[9]

Beginning in 1966, the Follett Publishing Company of Chicago began publishing his series, Discovering Music Together. Leonhard was chief editor of the series; Beatrice Perham Krone, Irving W. Wolfe, and Margaret Fullerton served with him on the editorial committee. With books for

California; Leonhard; Janet M. McGaughey, The University of Texas; Arrand Parsons, Northwestern University; William Thomson, Indiana University; Everett Timm, Louisiana State University; and Evelyn White, Howard University. Their recommendations are in "Recommendations of Group II: Musical Analysis and Aural Skills," in *Comprehensive Musicianship: The Foundation for College Education in Music* (Washington, DC: Music Educators National Conference, 1965), 14–17. Leonhard served briefly as a member of the Comprehensive Musicianship Project Policy Committee, from 1969–1970. See *Music Educators Journal* 59 (May 1973): 47.

[8]Frank Crockett, "Georgia Scene," *Georgia Music News* 26 (February 1966): 24.

[9]Leonhard spent a good bit of effort on the tapes, making ten trips to Atlanta to work on them for three or more days at a stretch. The four tapes, entitled "Discovery Through Listening," "Melody," "Rhythm," and "Harmony," exemplify Leonhard's belief in getting students involved with real music for experience and study. Unfortunately the tapes are now nowhere to be found. See Leonhard to Heller, 25 August 1993.

grades kindergarten through eighth grade, teachers' editions, recordings, and a teacher education book, the series was a practical, day-by-day working out for classroom teachers of the ideas Leonhard had presented at the various seminars and in the various publications.[10]

Beatrice Perham Krone (b. 1901) was on the faculty of the University of Southern California at the time the series came out. She and her husband, Max T. Krone, founded the Idyllwild School of Music and the Arts in 1950. They worked together on numerous publications, including a previous series for Follett, of which Max was the chief editor: Together We Sing (1951–64).[11]

Irving W. Wolfe (b. 1903) was Professor of Music at the George Peabody College for Teachers in Nashville, Tennessee when Follett published Discovering Music Together. He had worked with Margaret Fullerton and the Krones on Together We Sing and was a student of Charles A. Fullerton at the Iowa State Teachers College in Cedar

[10]Charles Leonhard, Beatrice Perham Krone, Irving Wolfe, and Margaret Fullerton, eds., Discovering Music Together, Vols. K–8 (Chicago: Follett Publishing Company, 1966–70). In addition to kindergarten through eighth grade books, Follett also issued teachers' editions, a set of recordings, and a teacher education book. Jay Hinshaw, Ruth Heller, and Marci Wyle served as in-house editors at Follett for the series. Sidney Fox, of the Follett Publishing Company in Chicago, was the consultant for the recordings and listening lessons. O. M. Hartsell of the University of Arizona served as a consultant for the seventh and eighth grade books. Charles R. Hoffer (then teaching in Clayton, Missouri, and later a president of the MENC) was a consultant on orchestral instruments. Gretchen Hieronymous (then with the laboratory school at Eastern Illinois University, later—as Gretchen Hieronymous Beall—one of Leonhard's doctoral students at the University of Illinois) and Robert B. Smith (who had completed his doctorate with Leonhard in 1961 was then employed as Associate Professor of Child Development and Music at the University of Illinois) also served as consultants for the series. Gloria Follett served as consultant for visual aids, Norman Baugher did the cover art and book designs, and James Yep provided the illustrations.

[11]Beatrice Perham Krone, Idyllwild, CA, to George N. Heller, Lawrence, KS, 8 July 1990, original in possession of the author. In addition to her work on music series books for Follett, Ms. Krone was involved in over forty publications either as sole author or co-author from 1937 until 1968. She had a special interest in music of countries around the world and integration of music and social studies.

Falls, now the University of Northern Iowa. Fullerton had developed a system of using recordings to teach elementary general music which could be used by classroom teachers. Wolfe had worked with Fullerton in this system before becoming involved with Together We Sing.[12]

At the time the Discovering Music Together series came out, Margaret Fullerton was music librarian at the University of Northern Iowa, in Cedar Falls. She held the copyright for the Fullerton-Wolfe Song Series, Together We Sing (1950 edition). When Charles Fullerton died in 1945, his daughter filed for the copyright of what was then called the Fullerton-Wolfe Song Series. Fullerton and Wolfe invited Beatrice Krone to join them, which she did in 1951. This was the edition which Follett published prior to Max Krone's involvement.[13]

The innovations in the Discovering Music Together series are immediately evident in the first book. First, the Leonhard series had many more songs: 102 as compared with 62 in Together We Sing. Second, 67 of the 102 songs in the first grade book of Discovering Music Together were in the teachers' edition, but not in the students' book. Third, special pages for teachers in the teachers' edition were more numerous, and they started right out by stating objectives in clear behavioral terms. Leonhard also provided text for the French folk tune, "Come and Play," and words and music for the song, "Halloween." In both instances, the credit went to D. L. McRae, but this was his mother's maiden name. One of the recordings for the first book features the

[12]Donald R. Goss, "Irving W. Wolfe: His Life and Contributions to Music Education" (Ph.D. diss., George Peabody College for Teachers, 1972), 1, 36–37, 42–43, 71–72, 91–93, 100, 113–115; and Irving Wolfe, "Rural School Music Missionary," *Music Educators Journal* 46 (April–May 1960): 26–28.

[13]Lewis R. Sheckler, "Charles Alexander Fullerton His Life and Contribution to Music Education" (Ed.D. diss., University of Illinois, 1965), 168–169, 180, 190–191; and Goss, "Irving W. Wolfe," 91–93, 100.

University of Illinois Concert Band, Mark Hindsley, Conductor, playing "Columbia, the Gem of the Ocean."[14]

In the second book, Leonhard et al. again offered behavioral objectives to teachers in the areas of music appreciation, musical competencies, and musical concepts. The newer book had 102 songs as compared with 96 in Together We Sing; 54 of these were new, and 48 were in both books. Listening examples in the recorded selections included some ethnic music and contemporary American composers along with the usual offering of traditional Western art music. A composition by Leonhard appears in Discovering Music Together, Book Two: "Halloween Night," words and music by D. L. McRae.[15]

Book Three in the new series had the usual list of objectives and a description of how the book was organized. As with the other books, the teachers' edition provided suggestions for how teachers could organize a lesson and present, teach, and lead a song. It also advised on how to teach rhythmic responsiveness and listening. The third grade book for Discovering Music Together had about the same number of songs as its predecessor (134 vs. 136 for the third grade book of Together We Sing); 57 were carried over, and 77 were new. Listening lessons include recorded selections by European masters and Aaron Copland, Heitor Villa-Lobos, Elie Siegmeister, and John Philip Sousa. Book three has yet another Halloween song by D. L. McRae: "Fun on Halloween."[16]  (See Figure 16.)

---

[14]Charles Leonhard, Beatrice Perham Krone, Irving Wolfe, and Margaret Fullerton, Discovering Music Together, Book One (Chicago: Follett Publishing Company, 1966), passim; and  Max T. Krone, Irving Wolfe, Beatrice Perham Krone, and Margaret Fullerton, *Music Round the Clock* (Chicago: Follett Publishing Company, 1955), passim.

[15]Leonhard, et al., Discovering Music Together, Book Two, passim; and Krone, et al., *Music Round the Town*, passim.

[16]Leonhard, et al., Discovering Music Together, Book Three, passim; and Krone, et al., *Music Through the Year*, passim.

## Figure 16

### "Fun on Halloween," by D. L. McRae*

# Fun on Halloween

D. L. M.

D. L. McRae

Witch-es and gob-lins on Hal - low - een!     (Rhythm echo)*
Gob - lins go fly - ing a - round the town;

So     man - y things you've nev - er seen!
Witch-es on broom-sticks swish a-round;

Of     all     the fun we have____ in the fall,
And ten black cats will get in - to a fight.

Hal - low - een time is best____ of ___ all.
We have great fun on Hal-low - een _night!

* Choose rhythm instruments to play the rhythm echoes.

▼
Many years ago there was a holiday on November 1 called "Summer's End."
It was a happy day.
But people believed that on the evening before the holiday the Moon God sent
bad things to earth. Fires were lit to scare away ghosts, elves, witches, and
their cats. This is how HALLOWEEN began.

*Leonhard, et al., Discovering Music Together, Book Three, 152.
Used by permission of Silver Burdett Ginn.

Discovering Music Together, Book Four, contains 117 songs, as compared with 157 in its predecessor. With forty fewer songs, it carried over 62 from the prior edition and added 55 new ones. Like the other books for the earlier grades, Book Four had advice to the teachers on how to evaluate instruction. The teachers' edition pointed out how evaluation was best if based on the stated objectives, and that it should be informal but systematic. It also recommended administering Part I of the *Elementary Music Achievement Test* also available from Follett, which Richard J. Colwell had written. Leonhard and his co-editors recommended using feedback from evaluation to modify teaching as needed and for teachers to realize that not all children learn at the same rate. Among the American composers included in the recordings for listening were R. Nathaniel Dett, and John Philip Sousa.[17]

Book Five of the Leonhard et al. series contains 130 songs, 32 fewer than the fifth grade book of Together We Sing. Of these, 58 songs appear in both books, while 72 are new to the later series. In addition to stating objectives, describing the series, and giving advice to teachers on presentation and evaluation, the teachers' manual for Book Five has special suggestions for each song interleaved between pages of the student book. New in Book Five is an introduction to the humanities. This book also has instrumental accompaniment parts for a few of the songs. Sousa's "Semper Fidelis" march is the only American composition in the recorded excerpts for listening.[18]

Discovering Music Together, Book Six, contains 136 songs, 58 of which are new. One of the new songs was a Leonhard favorite, "Charlie Is My Darling" (p. 80). The

[17]Leonhard, et al., Discovering Music Together, Book Four, passim; and Krone, et al., *Music Across Our Country*, passim.

[18]Leonhard, et al., Discovering Music Together, Book Five, passim; and Krone, et al., *Voices of America*, passim.

sixth grade book has a somewhat expanded section for accompanying instruments, string, wind, and percussion. Listening examples and recordings include music of Raymond Scott, Louis Moreau Gottschalk, Ulysses Kay, and Aaron Copland, among others.[19] The two books for junior high general music in the Discovering Music Together series are substantially different from their counterparts in the Together We Sing series. The seventh grade book in the Leonhard, et al. series contains 116 songs, only 21 of which appeared in the seventh grade book of the Krone et al. series, and the eighth grade book has 103 songs, of which only 22 are in the eighth grade book in the older series. Leonhard's books contain much advice on working with boys' changing voices and uncertain singers, and they contain considerably more information on music theory and music history. Book Seven also contains instructions for beginning recorder. The organization of Book Eight demonstrates functional and aesthetic values in music. Book Eight also contains a survey of music history. Whereas Books One through Six had three albums with song accompaniments and one album of recorded listening selections, Books Seven and Eight each had three albums of accompaniments and three albums for listening. Listening selections for Book Seven include works by Heitor Villa-Lobos, Aaron Copland, Edgar Varèse, Carlos Chávez, Morton Gould, and Ralph Matesky. Book Eight features selections by Leonard Bernstein, Aaron Copland, and Charles Ives. "The Origins and Development of Jazz" is a special supplementary record album for Book Eight.[20]

[19]Leonhard, et al., Discovering Music Together, Book Six, passim; and Krone, et al., *Voices of the World*, passim.

[20]Leonhard, et al., Discovering Music Together, Book Seven, passim; and Krone, et al., *Music Sounds Afar*, passim. The special album on jazz led to a very successful series, *The World of Popular Music*, a four-album set of listening lessons on rock, African-American music, jazz, and folk and country music which Sidney Fox and others developed for Follett in 1975.

The series appeared in a revised form in 1970. The revised series included a new book on early childhood, which was largely the work of Robert B. Smith. It also featured a new listening album on "Folk Instruments of the World." The junior high books underwent substantial revision, changing both form and content. Discovering Music Together, Book Seven, became *Elements and Style*, and it had a totally revamped structure emphasizing folk and popular music, jazz, and electronic and experimental music. New recordings present performances by Pete Seeger, Donovan (Leitch), The Byrds, Curtis Mayfield, and the University of Illinois Jazz Band. Discovering Music Together, Book Eight, became *Our Musical Heritage*, stressing the elements, uses and functions of music, and music history.[21]

In 1971, Follett brought out a teacher education edition of Discovering Music Together. Co-authors for this edition included Leonhard, Krone, Wolfe and Fullerton and Robert B. Smith, who was formerly a consultant on the series. This publication consisted of a book for students in music teacher education methods classes and a two-record album of excerpts from recordings of the series. The book had four sections. "Let's Make Music" contains limited range songs and expanded range songs. "Music in Early Childhood" features listening, performing and creating activities built around musical elements. "Music in Middle Childhood" continues the work of the previous section with additional instruction on playing the recorder and ideas for teaching music as part of a related arts program. "Let's Read Music"

---

[21]Charles Leonhard, Beatrice Perham Krone, Irving Wolfe, and Margaret Fullerton, *Discovering Music Together: Elements and Style*, Revised Edition (Chicago: Follett Educational Corporation, 1970), passim; and Charles Leonhard, Beatrice Perham Krone, Irving Wolfe, and Margaret Fullerton, *Discovering Music Together: Our Musical Heritage*, Revised Edition (Chicago: Follett Educational Corporation, 1970), passim.

takes students through the reading program embodied in the series.[22]

The Discovering Music Together series made the ideas Leonhard had about aesthetic education tangible and accessible to music teachers and to classroom teachers. His next project would also make the ideas Leonhard had about aesthetic education tangible and accessible, this time to graduate students and their teachers. His series, Contemporary Perspectives in Music Education, was very influential in bringing several promising young writers to the attention of the profession. As a result, graduate study in music education acquired a body of literature that went beyond everyday matters of how to work with the changing voice, prepare a band for a contest, or get string players into third position.

As he was winding up work on Discovering Music Together, Leonhard turned to his next task: to edit the series of books called Contemporary Perspectives in Music Education for Prentice-Hall, Inc. In 1970, Prentice-Hall was in the process of completing publication of Allen P. Britton's Foundations of Music Education Series (1966–1971), and the editorial office at Prentice-Hall was in a somewhat confused state due to acquisition of the company by a conglomerate. Thus Leonhard's series came out a year before Britton's had concluded. Music educators were the beneficiaries of this situation, having a total of twelve books, six in each series, at hand for reference and consultation.[23]

[22]Charles Leonhard, Beatrice Perham Krone, Irving Wolfe, Margaret Fullerton, and Robert B. Smith, Discovering Music Together, Teacher Education Edition (Chicago: Follett Educational Corporation, 1971), passim.

[23]Britton to Heller, 18 February, 1989. The books in the Britton series were Harriet Nordholm, *Singing in the Elementary Schools* (1966); Emil A. Holz and Roger E. Jacobi, *Teaching Band Instruments to Beginners* (1966); Elizabeth A. H. Green, *Teaching Stringed Instruments in Classes* (1966); Paul R. Lehman, *Tests and Measurements in Music* (1968); Marguerite V. Hood, *Teaching Rhythm and Classroom Instruments* (1970); and Frances M. Andrews, *Junior High General Music* (1971).

Each book in Leonhard's series had a foreword in which he briefly described the areas of knowledge (philosophy, psychology, and research methods) and processes (program development, instruction, administration, supervision, and evaluation) of music education. He noted that he and the other authors intended that the series be used in undergraduate music teacher education classes, though many reviewers found them to be more appropriate for graduate students.

The first three books came out in 1970. These included *The Evaluation of Music Teaching and Learning* by Richard J. Colwell, *A Philosophy of Music Education* by Bennett Reimer, and *Experimental Research in Music* by Clifford K. Madsen and Charles H. Madsen, Jr. Leonhard's foreword for each book contained some material which was common to all books in the series and some which commented on the unique aspects of each book.

For Colwell's book on evaluation, Leonhard wrote that the topic was a long-time interest of Colwell. "The fact that he began this quest as a graduate student in music education at the University of Illinois is a source of great personal and professional satisfaction to me."[24]  Leonhard, who had himself earlier written on this topic in the NSSE *Yearbook* of 1958, observed that evaluation was a traditional area of weakness in music education and music teacher preparation.

Colwell established the distinction between evaluation and measurement, and he cited the 1959 edition of *Foundations and Principles of Music Education*, by Leonhard and House on the importance of the aesthetic qualities of the musical experience. He also quoted Leonhard and House directly on guidelines for reliability. George Kyme reviewed Colwell's book for the *Journal of*

---

[24]Charles Leonhard, foreword to *The Evaluation of Music Teaching and Learning*, by Richard J. Colwell (Englewood Cliffs, NJ: Prentice-Hall, Inc., 1970), vi.

*Research in Music Education*, calling it "the most useful guide to music testing currently available."[25]

In the foreword to Reimer's *A Philosophy of Music Education*, Leonhard wrote that Reimer's basic premise was that a study of the nature and value of music was a necessary prologue to a philosophy of music education and that Reimer took on this task while also pointing out the implications of theory for practice. Leonhard called the book "a distinguished work which is relevant to all levels and specializations in music education."[26]

Reimer borrowed his conception of the four elements which are necessary to produce both a symbol and expressive form (subject, object, symbol or form, and the conception of the object given by the symbol) from the 1959 edition of Leonhard and House. Reimer did not cite Leonhard and House in suggestions for further reading at the end of any chapter, and Leonhard's name does not appear in the index. In a lengthy and thorough review, Abraham A. Schwadron said that "*A Philosophy of Music Education* provides a highly-charged, means-ends foundation for music education that can be realized by concerned and effective action."[27]

In his second edition, published in 1989, Reimer was more generous in acknowledging the contributions of his teacher. He noted that the 1958 NSSE *Yearbook* and Leonhard and House, *Foundations and Principles of Music*

[25]George Kyme, review of *The Evaluation of Music Teaching and Learning*, by Richard J. Colwell, in *Journal of Research in Music Education* 19 (Fall 1971): 381. See also Colwell, *The Evaluation of Music Teaching*, 9, 37.

[26]Charles Leonhard, foreword to *A Philosophy of Music Education*, by Bennett Reimer (Englewood Cliffs, NJ: Prentice-Hall, Inc., 1970), x.

[27]Abraham A. Schwadron, review of *A Philosophy of Music Education*, by Bennett Reimer, in *Journal of Research in Music Education* 19 (Summer 1971): 255. See also, Reimer, *A Philosophy of Music Education*, 58; and Leonhard and House, *Foundations and Principles of Music Educations* (1959), 84–85.

*Education*, "were the first scholarly attempts to forge a justification and an identity for music education beyond the dimensions of the recreational and the extra-musical." Reimer also said that "It was then that we began to understand ourselves to be primarily a vehicle for aesthetic education—the education of aesthetic sensitivity to the art of music."[28]

In the foreword to Madsen and Madsen, *Experimental Research in Music*, Leonhard said that the authors treated the concepts and techniques basic to experimental research and that their book was remarkable for clarity and comprehensiveness and for a refreshing and highly readable style. "I shall never forget the occasion of my first reading of this book in manuscript. Having grown accustomed to treatises on research being dull and pedantic, I was amazed and delighted to find myself reading a book on research that was interesting, witty, and down-to-earth, but at the same time filled with information and insights for the beginning researcher in music."[29] The Madsen brothers cited nothing from Leonhard and House nor from anything else Leonhard had written.

This book had an interesting developmental process. Clifford Madsen first wrote it for a class he was teaching in the fall of 1966. He then sent it to his brother, Charles, who was teaching at the University of Illinois at that time. Charles checked it through and edited the second part. Clifford Madsen  continued to use the book in mimeograph form in

[28]Bennett Reimer, *A Philosophy of Music Education*, 2nd ed. (Englewood Cliffs, NJ: Prentice Hall, 1989), 219. The footnote gives Leonhard and House credit for efforts which "reached a new height of sophistication under the impetus of the reform movement of the 1960s—a level that may well serve as the ideal for our profession for many years to come." This is the only mention Reimer makes of Leonhard in the second edition.

[29]Charles Leonhard, foreword to *Experimental Research in Music*, by Clifford K. Madsen and Charles H. Madsen, Jr. (Englewood Cliffs, NJ: Prentice-Hall, Inc., 1970), vi.

his classes, making revisions based on student feedback. In early 1968, the two authors submitted the book to Allyn and Bacon, Inc., where editors rejected it. Next, they sent it to Prentice-Hall, where it received similar treatment. In March 1968, Leonhard, who had somehow obtained a copy of the manuscript, called Madsen to say he had just read the manuscript and wanted to include it in his series, and Madsen accepted. An unnamed reviewer provided Leonhard with criticism which he relayed to Madsen in June of 1968. Madsen made some revisions and resubmitted the work in July of 1968.[30]

In 1971, Prentice-Hall brought out the fourth volume in Leonhard's series, Edwin E. Gordon's seminal work, *The Psychology of Music Teaching.* In the foreword, Leonhard noted Gordon's dual role as a teacher and researcher and how that helped him bring a unique and exceptionally valid point of view to the work. Gordon, Leonhard wrote, synthesized past research and proposed a learning theory which would help music teachers develop teaching practices that were psychologically sound. The book contains no citations from Leonhard and House nor from any of Leonhard's other writing.[31]

The series concluded in 1973 with two books, one by Leonhard's former student and co-author, Robert W. House, and the other by Robert G. Sidnell. In the foreword to House's book, *Administration in Music Education*, Leonhard said that all music educators were involved in administration to some degree and that House was a master both of its theory and practice. The book imparts both the

---

[30]Charles Leonhard, Urbana, IL to Professors Clifford and Charles Madsen, Tallahassee, FL, 21 June 1968, photocopy in possession of the author; Clifford K. Madsen and Charles H. Madsen, Tallahassee, FL, to Charles Leonhard, Urbana, IL, 22 July 1968, photocopy in possession of the author; and Clifford K. Madsen, Tallahassee, FL, to George N. Heller, Lawrence, KS, 24 October 1990, original in possession of the author.

[31]Charles Leonhard, foreword to *The Psychology of Music Teaching*, by Edwin E. Gordon (Englewood Cliffs, NJ: Prentice-Hall, Inc., 1971), x.

knowledge and the skills needed to succeed in music education administration. House's book is an expansion of Chapter Nine of the 1972 edition of *Foundations and Principles of Music Education*. House also cites Leonhard and House on music teacher supervision and objectives.[32]

Sidnell's, *Building Instructional Programs in Music Education* (1973) was the concluding work in the series. In the foreword, Leonhard noted that Sidnell was concerned with the process of program development and that his work was relevant to demands for accountability which was starting to concern music educators in the early 1970s. Sidnell helped delineate objectives and select experiences in music, and he attempted to bridge the gap between behavioristic and humanistic points of view toward the music education program. Sidnell cited the 1959 edition of Leonhard and House on the need for a philosophy of music education and on the need for program evaluation. He also acknowledged the contribution of Leonhard and House on guidelines for program evaluation.[33]

James Hanshumaker reviewed Sidnell's book for the *Journal of Research in Music Education*. He noted that Sidnell's work was a part of the Leonhard series and commended Leonhard's contributions to the profession, not only in this series but in his work with House on *Foundations and Principles*. Hanshumaker concluded that Sidnell's book "could and should be read by experienced

[32]Charles Leonhard, foreword to *Administration in Music Education*, by Robert W. House (Englewood Cliffs, NJ: Prentice-Hall, Inc., 1973), ix. See also House, *Administration in Music Education*, 38–39, 52–53, and 71.

[33]Charles Leonhard, foreword to *Building Instructional Programs in Music Education*, by Robert G. Sidnell (Englewood Cliffs, NJ: Prentice-Hall, 1973), vi. See also Sidnell, *Building Instructional Programs in Music Education*, 28, 136, and 143–144.

music teachers as well [as by graduate students], regardless of their areas of specialization."[34]

It is difficult to estimate the impact of this series on the growth and development of the music education profession. No doubt it was immense, and Leonhard's role as editor of a series of books a younger generation of scholars and practitioners in the field would read very carefully was crucial. The availability of these resources helped still younger students in the field to understand more clearly what the underpinnings of the profession consisted of, and the books helped guide them toward their own maturation as scholars in the field. It is significant that two of the books, Reimer's *A Philosophy of Music Education* and Madsen and Madsen's *Experimental Research in Music*, are still in print in revised editions. Many music education professors use them still as textbooks for courses in philosophy of music education and in research methods.

In addition to editing Discovering Music Together and Contemporary Perspectives in Music Education, Leonhard served the profession as a member of the Editorial Committee of the *Music Educators Journal* from 1968 to 1972. He also continued to write for a variety of other publications in the late 1960s and early 1970s. His works covered topics such as future directions in the field, developing researchers in music education, aesthetic education, and music in higher education.

In the spring of 1966, and again in September of 1968, Leonhard turned his pen toward prognostication. In an article in the Spring 1966 issue of the *Bulletin of the Council for Research in Music Education*, Leonhard wrote of the developing curriculum reform movement, the emphasis on structure of subject matter disciplines, and the increasing use

---

[34]James R. Hanshumaker, review of *Building Instructional Programs in Music Education*, by Robert G. Sidnell, in *Journal of Research in Music Education* 22 (Winter 1974): 330–331.

of subject matter specialists in the elementary school. He also noted the increasing emphasis on measurement and testing in education, the rise of a musical tradition and repertoire rooted in the society and culture, and the expanding role of the Federal Government in financial support of education and of the arts and humanities. Paraphrasing a Bob Dylan song made popular by Peter, Paul and Mary in 1963, Leonhard noted that "The winds of change are blowing strong in American schools."[35]

Leonhard spoke on this topic of change in the future of music education at the 1968 MENC convention in Seattle. His remarks, published in the September 1968 issue of the *Music Educators Journal*, alerted music educators to changes likely to take place in the 1970s. He talked about an emphasis on musicianship and a change from emphasis on activities to emphasis on experience. He called for more attention to the application of learning theory to music instruction, and he pointed out the trend toward increasing attention to music in early childhood. He noted the increasing operation of the elementary school music program within the framework of the self-contained classroom and the development and widespread adoption of a program of music in general education at the high school level. Leonhard concluded that "We can anticipate that music education will come to terms with the music of the twentieth century and with the role that music plays in the lives of the new generation."[36]

In 1967, Leonhard joined with Allen P. Britton of Michigan and Paul R. Lehman, then at the University of Kentucky, to present a paper at a conference on research in music education. The paper was on "Developing

[35]Charles Leonhard, "The Next Ten Years in Music Education," *Bulletin of the Council for Research in Music Education* 7 (Spring 1966): 14.

[36]Charles Leonhard, "The Next Ten Years," *Music Educators Journal* 55 (September 1968): 50.

Researchers in Music Education." Leonhard, Britton, and Lehman observed that graduate programs in music education date back to the 1930s. While most of these graduate programs traditionally culminated in a research project, they were more concerned with preparing teachers, performance, and service. The three authors noted changing circumstances in the field as more music educators studied to become researchers and teach research in music education. They also wrote on problems associated with recruitment and selection of researchers and the preparation of research specialists. Leonhard, Britton, and Lehman concluded their paper by pointing out the need to prepare consumers of research.[37]

In March of 1967, Leonhard spoke before the Western Division convention of the MENC in Las Vegas, Nevada. His remarks appeared in the April 1968 issue of the *Music Educators Journal* under the title, "Human Potential and the Aesthetic Experience." Leonhard addressed the importance of themes in the history of music education such as "Music for Every Child and Every Child *for* Music" (the motto of the MENC), and "Music and Academic Discipline" (a phrase very much in vogue following the Sputnik crisis of the late 1950s). He also talked about music as an aesthetic discipline, an idea which would come to fruition in later years as Discipline Based Art Education. "Every music educator must project an image of a sensitive, intelligent person who believes in and values the power and beauty of the art of music. Only then can we fulfill our mission as

[37]Charles Leonhard, Allen P. Britton, and Paul R. Lehman, "Developing Researchers in Music Education," in *A Conference on Research in Music Education*, ed. Henry L. Cady (Columbus, OH: The Ohio State University, 1967), 34–38.

music educators—to touch the hearts, stir the feelings, and kindle the imaginations of our students."[38]

Leonhard returned to this theme in October of 1970 in one of the keynote addresses at the Fourth Annual Conference in Music Education at Springfield, Illinois. He spoke on "Aesthetic Education in a World of Numbers." In his address, Leonhard noted the prevalence of numbers in modern life and the tendency to standardize behavior that often accompanies it. This emphasis on numbers and the concomitant standardization often leads to dulling or numbing of affect and to dropouts from school and from society or life itself. In such a world music education and its emphasis on qualitative considerations, creative responses, and aesthetic freedom becomes increasingly important. Leonhard lamented that many people were exaggerating and misconstruing ideas he had proposed over the past twenty years. His notions were simple and direct. Music education as aesthetic education was about "feeling, the stirring of it, the expression of it, the freeing of it through musical experience."[39]

Leonhard, together with one of his students, addressed yet another audience on music education: people in the general field of education. In 1971, The Macmillan Company and the Free Press, in cooperation with the Crowell-Collier Educational Corporation, put out *The Encyclopedia of Education*. In a comprehensive, though

[38] Charles Leonhard, "Human Potential and the Aesthetic Experience," *Music Educators Journal* 54 (April 1968): 111.

[39] Charles Leonhard, "Aesthetic Education in a World of Numbers," in *Fourth Annual Statewide Leadership Conference in Music Education: Summary Report* (Springfield, IL: Office of the Superintendent of Public Instruction, State of Illinois, 1971), 32. He gave essentially the same speech again at the annual convention of the Canadian Music Educators Association held in Charlottetown, Prince Edward Island, in the spring of 1971. See Charles Leonhard, "Aesthetic Education in a World of Numbers," *The Canadian Music Educator* 12 (Summer 1971): 5–7; and Charles Leonhard, "Aesthetic Education in a World of Numbers," *The British Columbia Music Educator* 15 (October 1971): 34–37.

brief, survey of many topics pertaining to teaching and learning, the encyclopedia included a series of articles under the general title of "Music Education." One of these, by Leonhard and Gary R. Sudano, dealt with music in higher education.[40]

Leonhard and Sudano summarized the history of music in higher education, beginning with the Boston Academy of Music in 1832. They described programs and enrollments and noted the three traditions of music in American higher education which had their roots in conservatories, liberal arts institutions, and teachers colleges. They wrote briefly on degrees and curriculum and programs in music theory, composition, and music history and musicology. They addressed issues connected with teaching applied music, music ensembles, and sacred music. They surveyed music therapy and music-teacher education, and they wrote of undergraduate and graduate programs in music. The article concluded with a discussion of professional organizations and trends and a brief bibliography.[41]

Back home in Illinois, Leonhard continued to teach classes, mostly at the masters and doctoral level. Fifty-one of his students in the years from 1965 to 1974 wrote doctoral dissertations on teaching music in higher education, general music, historical topics, instrumental music methods, program evaluation, programmed learning, choral music education, musical analysis, string education, computer assisted instruction in music, and the philosophy

[40]*The Encyclopedia of Education*, 1971 ed., s.v. "Music Education: 1. Elementary Schools," by O. M Hartsell; "Music Education: 2. Secondary Schools," by Richard J. Colwell; "Music Education: 3. Colleges," by Charles Leonhard and Gary R. Sudano; "Music Education: 4. Jazz," by M. E. Hall; "Music Education: 5. Education of American Composers," by Grant Beglarian; "Music Education: 6. Training of Teachers," by Robert H. Klotman; "Music Education: 7. Supervision in the Schools," by Charles L. Gary; "Music Education: 8. Evaluation," by Paul R. Lehman; and "Music Education: 8. Changing Goals," by Charles B. Fowler.

[41]*The Encyclopedia of Education*, 1971 ed., s.v. "Music Education: 3. Colleges," by Charles Leonhard and Gary R. Sudano.

of music education.[42]  (See the Appendix for a complete listing of the students' names and the titles of their dissertations.)

As the hopes and dreams of the Kennedy-Johnson years faded into the economic and other problems associated with the Nixon-Ford years, Leonhard continued to work for more unification of theory and practice in the pursuit of aesthetic education.  Having provided materials for teachers and books and articles for scholars, he would turn his attention increasingly to the problems inherent in music teacher education in the years to come.  He believed more and more that the undergraduate music teacher education program provided the best opportunities for leaders to intervene for change and improvement in music education generally.

[42]The numbers of students completing doctoral dissertations under Leonhard's supervision in these years were four in 1965, three in 1966, five in 1967, three in 1968, six in 1969, five in 1970, six in 1971, eight in 1972, eight in 1973, and four in 1974.

# CHAPTER VII

# MUSIC TEACHER EDUCATION

As the 1970s passed and the 1980s arrived, Leonhard began to contemplate closing out his career at the University of Illinois and preparing for life in retirement. The years were passing quickly, but this seems to have had little, if any, effect on him. He continued to teach graduate courses, supervise doctoral dissertations, write articles, give speeches, and participate in symposiums around the country with the same energy and enthusiasm he had always given to these activities. At this point in his career, Leonhard began to observe that teacher education in general and music teacher education in particular were experiencing considerable turmoil. Declining college student populations combined with shrinking resources and increased demands made preparing music teachers a difficult and demanding task.

Leonhard had made major contributions in professional writing and editing and in teaching, but he had yet to tackle the social and political problems associated with music teacher education in a direct way. As he looked at the trends which were developing and reflected on his long advocacy of aesthetic education, he saw a need to act in behalf of music teacher educators. Perhaps this could be his swan song, so to speak, as his own career in higher education at the University of Illinois drew to a close.

Leonhard renewed his interest in prognostication in the mid-1970s with an article, "Trends in the Future of Music Education." The article was originally an address to the Wisconsin Music Educators Association convention, and it attracted the attention of editors in several other states, as well. In this essay he noted the changes in society and music over the preceding ten years. He also observed the rise of behaviorism in American education and a countervailing turn toward humanism. He saw the profession as one in conflict: "Never in my 37 years of experience has the music education program been so segmented and so obsessed by processes, many of which are contradictory to one another, as it is today."[1]

Leonhard boldly set forth twelve predictions for the coming decade. He forecast an increasing emphasis on the affective potential of music with comprehensive musicianship providing the focus for music education from the kindergarten through college. He predicted the accommodation of music education and the concept of accountability and foresaw an increasing emphasis on creativity. Leonhard thought there would probably be more programs for musically gifted students and greater attention given to music in special education. He prognosticated that music educators would offer more mini-courses on musical topics in secondary schools, and he saw a coming expansion of the kinds of music performance opportunities for children which might include such things as country and western music groups, Mariachi bands, and balalaika orchestras.[2]

Leonhard wrote that music education programs were likely to offer more varied delivery systems—large group,

[1]Charles Leonhard, "Trends in the Future of Music Education," *The Nebraska Music Educator* 33 (April 1975): 2. See also, Charles Leonhard, "Trends in the Future of Music Education," *The Illinois Music Educator* 36 (Summer 1976): 8.

[2]Leonhard, "Trends in the Future of Music Education," [*Nebraska Music Educator*], 11.

small group, and individual—and he looked forward to a greater degree of unity as music educators came to accept the idea of comprehensive musicianship. As he saw it, the situation looked good for more music administrative positions, especially in large school systems. Finally, Leonhard thought that music educators would probably continue or possibly even strengthen their tradition of approaching the subject with passion. This he heartily endorsed: ". . . if I have to choose between talent and passion or intelligence and passion, I will take passion every time."[3]

In the mid-1960s, Leonhard had become involved with the Aesthetic Education Program (AEP) of the Central Midwest Regional Education Laboratory, Inc. (CEMREL). He was connected in one way or another with CEMREL during the course of its existence from the mid-1960s until it ceased operations in the 1980s. He also served on the AEP Advisory Board from 1969 until 1976. Leonhard's association with this group provided many opportunities for students in music education at the University of Illinois to become involved in its activities, as well as providing opportunities for his ideas and experiences to the benefit of CEMREL and the AEP.[4]

In the summer of 1976, CEMREL joined with the Education Program of the Aspen Institute for Humanistic Studies and the National Institute of Education in putting a conference entitled "The Arts and Aesthetics: An Agenda for the Future." As part of their contribution to the conference and its subsequent publication, Leonhard and Richard

---

[3]Leonhard, "Trends in the Future of Music Education," [*Nebraska Music Educator*], 11.

[4]Leonhard to Heller, 4 August 1993. See also, Stanley S. Madeja, "The Aesthetics of Education: The CEMREL Aesthetic Education Program," *Bulletin of the Council for Research in Music Education* 43 (Summer 1975): 1–18; and Bernard S. Rosenblatt and Rene Michel-Trapaga, "Through the Teacher to the Child: Aesthetic Education for Teachers," *Bulletin of the Council for Research in Music Education* 43 (Summer 1975): 46–47.

Colwell presented an essay on "Research in Music Education."[5]

In their presentation at Aspen, Leonhard and Colwell noted the conflicts between science and art and the limited number of people actually qualified to do research in music education. They gave a brief history of music education research and told the story of funded research in the 1960s. The two authors systematically reviewed, however briefly, studies on music teaching and learning, and they surveyed studies on musical development and maturation. They looked at research on training and attitudes, and they gave capsule summaries of research on perception and psychoacoustics. They mentioned studies on what was then called automated learning, and they discussed emerging investigations in the fields of creativity and psychological theory.

Leonhard and Colwell closed their contribution to the conference with some suggestions for the future. In addition to offering some questions they thought were important for music educators to study, they called for more research which could lead to formulation of testable theories. They urged investigators to pursue studies over time, and they pointed out the need for financial support for music education research. Leonhard and Colwell concluded their remarks by calling for development of professional research corps in music education whose primary mission would be to do research and publish the results.[6]

[5]Charles Leonhard and Richard J. Colwell, "Research in Music Education," in *Arts and Aesthetics: An Agenda for the Future* , ed. Stanley S. Madeja (St. Louis, MO: CEMREL, Inc., 1977), 81–108. See also Charles Leonhard and Richard J. Colwell, "Research in Music Education," *Bulletin of the Council for Research in Music Education* 49 (Winter 1976): 1–30.

[6]The twelve questions Leonhard and Colwell proposed were: What is music as art? What constitutes aesthetic responsiveness to music? How does aesthetic responsiveness to music relate to aesthetic responsiveness to other arts? What is the basis for aesthetic responsiveness to music? What is the basis for musical perception? What is the influence of aptitude on the development of musical responsiveness and perception? What is the

In the fall of 1979, the *Bulletin of the Council for Research in Music Education* published a fifteen-year retrospective of the 1963 Yale Seminar. The issue featured comments by many of the participants, most of whom had rather positive things to say about it. Leonhard had not participated in the original meeting, but he had followed its deliberations closely and was well aware of its consequences. He especially noted the role the Seminar played in eliciting criticism of the profession—albeit by outsiders, most of whom were from the northeastern United States. Leonhard wrote of the call for an expanded repertoire and greater emphasis on creativity which the Seminar engendered. He noted the recommendations for a sequential listening program and activities and courses for advanced students. He commented on the call for musicians in residence in the schools, more utilization of community resources, and high schools of performing arts. He noted the recommendations for teaching aids and the proposal to use performance experience as the basis for musical learning. He underlined the recommendation for more elementary general music specialists and the recommendation that music be considered a subject meriting serious study. Leonhard concluded that the Seminar was probably worthwhile, especially for those who participated in it directly.[7]

---

influence of maturation on the development of musical responsiveness and perception? To what extent can a growth gradient be established for the development of musical responsiveness and perception? How can aptitude for musical responsiveness and perception be measured? How does achievement of performance skills, listening skills, and skill in analyzing compositional devices and stylistic characteristics affect the development of musical responsiveness and perception? What types of experience with music contribute to the development of musical responsiveness and perception? See Leonhard and Colwell, "Research in Music Education" [in Madeja, ed., *Arts and Aesthetics*], 99–100.

[7]Charles Leonhard, "Was the Yale Seminar Worthwhile?" *Bulletin of the Council for Research in Music Education* 60 (Fall 1979): 61–64.

In January of 1981, Leonhard addressed the members of the Missouri Music Educators Association meeting in their annual convention. He spoke on the confusion between means and ends in music education. He told the music educators in his audience that "We have come to the place where we emphasize the means to the expressive import of music at the expense of the expressive import itself."[8] This process, he said, begins early in the program and continues throughout elementary and secondary schools and in colleges and universities. It is true in listening and in performing activities. "We must realize that the appropriate subject matter of music study is music itself."[9]

Leonhard suggested to the Missouri music teachers that they simplify their programs and choose music that is attractive to children. He recommended that they emphasize phrasing and introduce information about the music only as needed. To instrumental teachers he gave the advice that true musical technique involves expressiveness and that they should provide experiences in expressiveness from the very beginning. He thought all students could benefit from more playing by ear. To conductors of performing groups in Missouri he issued a challenge to choose repertoire within the technical proficiency of students so that they could work on the music, not just the notes. Leonhard also urged them to work more often on sight-reading. He encouraged conductors to play exemplary recordings for their groups and involve students directly in all aspects of music. In closing he reminded the Missouri music educators that "responsiveness to music is taught by example and learned by contagion."[10]

[8]Charles Leonhard, "The Great Masquerade: Means Become Ends," *Missouri School Music Magazine* 35 (Spring 1981): 30.

[9]Ibid., 31.

[10]Ibid., 40.

In February of 1981, Leonhard was one of the featured speakers at the Loyola Music Symposium IV: Music in Community Education, sponsored by the music department at Loyola University in New Orleans, Louisiana. On this occasion, he addressed his concerns for broadening music education to include more than simply students in schools, grades kindergarten through twelve. He spoke on the topic of "Lifelong Learning in Music: A Challenge to Music Educators." Leonhard's talk reviewed the history of music education from the singing-school of the eighteenth century through the community singing movement of the early twentieth century which featured the work of Peter W. Dykema, whom he had known at Teachers College.[11]

The social, cultural, and economic circumstances of the late twentieth century made community music once again an important part of the music education professional agenda. Leonhard saw this as an opportunity for music educators to be more inclusive in their work. He saw the chance for music educators to contribute to making America a musical nation by changing their attitudes about who their clientele should be. He also saw this situation as calling for music educators to back away from increasing specialization and narrowness. His remarks at the Loyola Symposium offered a practical ten-point program for music educators who might be interested in this activity.[12]

In the late spring of 1981, The University of Illinois School of Music held a symposium to commemorate the establishment of the doctoral program in music education. While the organizers of the program dedicated it to Duane Branigan, who had been Director of the School of Music from 1950 to 1971, in many respects it was a tribute to the

[11]Charles Leonhard, "Lifelong Learning in Music: A Challenge to Music Educators," in *Loyola Music Symposium IV: Music in Community Education*, ed. David Swanzy and William S. English (New Orleans, LA: Loyola University, 1981), 33–39.

[12]Leonhard, "Lifelong Learning in Music," 36–39.

career and impending retirement of Charles Leonhard. Richard J. Colwell edited the book of proceeding of the Symposiums, subtitled *A Festschrift for Charles Leonhard*. The dedication of that publication featured a 1951 picture of Leonhard and a tribute in which Colwell wrote that "It was Professor Leonhard's leadership that placed the University of Illinois in its preeminent position."[13]   In response, Leonhard told the 107 participants, most of whom had written their doctoral dissertations under his supervision: "I ask only that you continue to commit yourselves to the human values of music education and that you develop in your students a commitment to use music to fulfill the mission of the true music educator—*to bring beauty into the lives of people.*"[14]

It was in the proceedings of this 1981 Symposium that Leonhard first published his program to reform music teacher education. He began with a tribute to the success of American music teacher education and a brief survey of its history. He followed with a description of the status of music teacher education as it existed in the early 1980s at both the undergraduate and graduate levels. He commented at some length on the inservice education of music teachers and identified some recent developments that might impinge on music teacher education. He closed his essay with a list of problems: lack of systematic development, narrowness, resistance to innovation, limited views of faculty, lack of basic research, and lack of participation by the music establishment (composers, theorists, musicologists,

---

[13]Richard J. Colwell, "Dedication," in *Symposium in Music Education: A Festschrift for Charles Leonhard* (Urbana, IL: University of Illinois, 1982), i.

[14]"Details on the 1981 Symposium in Music Education," in *Symposium in Music Education*, v. Italics in the original.

conductors, professional performers, and critics) in music teacher education.[15]

Leonhard followed his January 1981 article on means and ends in music education for Missouri music educators with another for Florida music educators in December. This second article appeared in the *Florida Music Educator*. Leonhard was scheduled to be the keynote speaker at the annual meeting of the Florida Music Educators Association in January, 1982 in Daytona Beach. His article on means and ends appeared just a month prior in the Association's journal.[16]

The marching band was the most extreme example of confusing means and ends in music education, Leonhard said in his article. He assailed both the proponents of the marching band who hold it to be central to the music program and the critics of marching bands who believe it belongs in the athletic department, not the music department. "For the first group the marching band is an end in itself; for the second, it is a means to nothing."[17] Though marching bands might exemplify this problem most dramatically, all performing groups shared in the confusion of means and ends to some degree. The solution, he said, was for "band, orchestra, and choral rehearsals [to] become music laboratories in which students study and understand the music they play."[18] The music program should include such experiences for children, but only as a part of the total music curriculum, "sequentially organized from grade to grade and

[15]Charles Leonhard, "Music Teacher Education in the United States," in *Symposium in Music Education*, 233–247.

[16]Charles Leonhard, "Means and Ends in Music Education," *Florida Music Director* 35 (December 1981): 10–11.

[17]Ibid., 10.

[18]Ibid.

level to level, moving inexorably toward the attainment of valid musical objectives."[19]

In his keynote speech to the Florida music educators, Leonhard spoke on the social significance of music education. He built his argument upon a premise asserting the social nature of the art of music, citing the uses and functions of music in world cultures. Music educators must come to understand the social significance of music and of music education if they are to be effective. He especially emphasized the value of music as a worthy use of leisure time. Music education must emphasize freedom and creativity: "We must forego elitism; we must abolish imposed standards of excellence, burdensome rules and organizational demands; we must root out regimentation and emphasize personal involvement and personalized and flexible definitions of success."[20]

Leonhard brought his ideas for reform of music teacher education before the profession at large in a dramatic fashion. In the fall of 1981, he broached his ideas to the Council for Institutional Cooperation at Michigan State University. Satisfied with his colleagues' response, he moved to get on the program of the Music Educators National Conference at San Antonio in February, 1982. Speaking before a packed room at the MENC, Leonhard identified the music teacher education program as a product of liberal arts colleges, conservatories, and teachers' colleges. He saw other forces involved, such as the academy (music history, music theory, and applied music) and accrediting agencies (the National Council for the Accreditation of Teacher Education, the National Association of Schools of Music [NASM], and state boards of education). MENC involvement, he said, was sporadic.

[19] Leonhard, "Means and Ends in Music Education," 11.

[20] Charles Leonhard, "Music Education: A Socially Significant Enterprise," *Florida Music Director* 35 (March 1982): 7.

The major initiatives had come from Marguerite Hood in the NASM fight of 1951, and later from Frances M. Andrews and Robert Klotman.[21]

Leonhard was in fine form on that February afternoon in San Antonio. He asserted that music teacher education suffers from a continuing lack of prestige and authority. He identified competency testing as the latest threat, with its threats to examine teachers at the entry level and in service. The game, he pointed out, is political, not academic. Though Leonhard had not often been officially involved with the MENC, nor with any other professional organization (a forty-year credo, he said), perhaps now was the time.[22]

Slippage in the dignity of the profession was a problem, and Leonhard expressed dismay about compartmentalization in music education. An organization of music teacher educators should be a unifying force rather than a divisive one. Thus, he proposed an organization of music teacher educators that would seek a place on the National Executive Board of the MENC and launch a publication. The group could mount an offensive and help facilitate communication. It could plan convention sessions and speak with an effective and authoritative voice to member schools, and to the NASM. At the session, Leonhard announced that he had written a letter to the National Executive Board requesting approval of a Council on Music Teacher Education.[23]

After Leonhard concluded his speech, he suggested that people in the room divide up into MENC divisions and elect a person from each division to serve on a steering committee. The caucuses took place immediately. Members

---

[21]George N. Heller, Handwritten notes taken at Charles Leonhard's speech to the Music Educators National Conference, 12 February 1982, San Antonio Texas, original in possession of the author.

[22]Ibid.

[23]Ibid.

of the North Central Division elected Robert Klotman, and people from the Eastern Division elected Donald Shetler. Southern Division music teacher educators named Irma Collins, and Northwestern Division members tabbed Marlon Tatum (Karin Yeskin later replaced her). Kansans at the meeting put forth the name of John W. Grashel, and he became the Southwestern representative. The Western Division people chose Phyllis Erwin. Leonhard met briefly with the six division representatives, and the meeting adjourned.[24]

In an immediate follow-up memo to persons attending the San Antonio meeting, Leonhard announced that the National Executive Board of the MENC had approved the Council for Music Teacher Education at its meeting in July, 1982. He noted that he would chair the Steering Committee and that it would meet at the CIC in Madison, Wisconsin in the fall of 1982. The Madison meeting was to take up issues relevant to music teacher education.[25]

Leonhard quickly followed up on his San Antonio presentation with a speech to the Kansas Council on Music Teacher Education Programs (KCOMTEP) at the Rock Springs Ranch, near Junction City, Kansas, on September 16, 1982. He once again asserted that music teacher education had been successful and required no apologies. He said, however, that it has produced too many ineffective and ill-prepared teachers. Music education has failed to attract musically talented and academically gifted students,

---

[24]Heller, Handwritten MENC notes.

[25]Charles Leonhard, Urbana, IL, Memorandum to Persons Attending the Session of the Council on Music Teacher Education at San Antonio, 2 August 1982, photocopy in possession of the author. The National Executive Board of the MENC approved formation of the Society for Music Teacher Education rather than a Council, as Leonhard had proposed. Nor did its members grant the Society a seat on the Board.

and those students who do go into music education suffer from the low esteem it has in academia.[26]

Leonhard told the Kansas music educators that music teacher education has changed little in the nearly fifty years since the Edna McEachern study of 1937. Music teacher education, he said, is not designed specifically to train music teachers. Conservatories, liberal arts colleges, and teachers colleges have contributed to an overgrown thicket of curricular offerings and requirements. The early emphasis was on performers and methods and on general education requirements. This has produced a hydra-headed monster.[27]

Leonhard surveyed the various strategies to deal with the problem. These include four-plus-one and five-year programs. These solutions maintain the hybrid nature of existing programs and sometimes amount to little more than manipulation of semester hours, The NASM has mandated a decline of music education hours from twenty-two percent to fifteen in the past fifty years. In the meantime, course requirements have proliferated, now totalling 135–140 hours with no electives.[28]

The pressures from outside the field—certification, mainstreaming, a decline in the pool of high school graduates, weak perceptions of music and music education among high school graduates—continue to mount. Music educators, Leonhard advised, must get off the defensive and quit reacting to demands of others. They must demand responsibility for planning music teacher education, and they must ignore "fusty" demands of the conservatory, the

[26]George N. Heller, Handwritten notes taken at Charles Leonhard's speech to the Kansas Council of Music Teacher Education Programs at Rock Springs Ranch, near Junction City, KS, 16 September 1982, handwritten on conference program, original in possession of the author.

[27]Ibid. The study to which Leonhard referred was Edna McEachern, *A Survey and Evaluation of the Education of School Music Teachers in the United States*, Teachers College Columbia Contribution to Education, No. 701 (New York: Teachers College, Columbia University, 1937).

[28]Heller, Handwritten KCOMTEP notes.

"specious" demands of liberal arts colleges, and pressures from various education groups.[29]

Leonhard outlined what he saw as the essential steps needed for effective reform. Music educators must define behaviors and select experiences. They must organize sequential and logical programs. Improvement is impossible without change. Music theory may not be necessary, or perhaps colleges and universities may have to teach it as part of a comprehensive package along with music history, and music education. It may be necessary to re-examine piano proficiency requirements and to decide if all students must study all instruments.[30]

The reform would have to involve more than just the music education faculty. The students also have a vital role to play. They must learn to analyze instruction and value theory. They need to acquire a basis for evaluation and develop some principles on which they can rely. They need to practice synthesis-analysis-synthesis teaching strategies and evaluate constantly. Students in music teacher education programs must acquire the cognitive skills which are so useful in teaching.[31]

To have a meaningful reform of music teacher education, music educators must reconcile theory and practice, not only philosophically, but also operationally. Instruction of the past is at fault in for not applying theory to practice. Educational psychology and foundations courses, where students should encounter this reconciliation of theory and practice, have had too little impact. Often music education professors do not demonstrate practice grounded

[29]Heller, Handwritten KCOMTEP notes.

[30]Ibid.

[31]Ibid.

in sound theory for their students and thus fail to provide them with good models.[32]

Leonhard called for a redefinition of music teacher education in which music teacher educators would be the specialists in the design and instruction of all phases of music. Music teacher educators should be involved in the analysis of process and product of their own programs. They should design their programs to fit the unique characteristics and circumstances of their particular institutions. They should modernize their instructional resources, including computer-assisted instruction and micro-processing, and they should offer opportunities for their students to participate in micro-teaching. They should modernize the music curriculum to include jazz, contemporary folk music, and popular music. Music teacher educators should encourage their students to develop interests outside of music and to relate music to society and culture. They should maintain a flexible program, making due allowances for students' abilities and professional aspirations.[33]

In October, Leonhard attended the meetings of the CIC in Madison, Wisconsin. At that time, he called for the Steering Committee of the Society for Music Teacher Education (SMTE) to meet. Following these meetings, he sent a memo to all who had attended the original meeting in San Antonio to report on what had transpired at Madison. The Steering Committee developed a plan to ask states to appoint SMTE chairs. Divisions would have SMTE chairs, and membership in the society would be voluntary by indication on the MENC membership application form. Chair and members of the Steering Committee agreed to develop bylaws. The Steering Committee proposed that state

[32]Heller, Handwritten KCOMTEP notes.
[33]Ibid.

chairs organize sessions at state meetings in 1982–83 and that division chairs organize sessions at division meetings in 1983. The national chair would prepare reports for the *Music Educators Journal*. The Steering Committee would encourage reprinting of the Klotman Commission report (1972) and would plan sessions for the MENC convention in Chicago in 1984. Leonhard chaired the Steering Committee which consisted of representatives from each of the six MENC divisions.[34]

In the fall of 1984, the University of Wisconsin held a Symposium on Teacher Education on the campus in Madison. Eunice Boardman, one of Leonhard's former students and his successor as Chair of the Society for Music Teacher Education, was Director of the School of Music at Wisconsin and hosted the Symposium. Gerald Olson, a professor in music education on the Wisconsin faculty, served as Chair of the National Task Force on Teacher Education. Olson was also the editor of the journal, *Dialogue in Instrumental Music Education*, which carried publications of the proceedings.[35]

Leonhard gave the keynote speech for the Madison Symposium. He spoke to the participants on methods courses, which he saw as critical to music teacher education. He said that students found them too theoretical, unrealistic, repetitious, and uninteresting. They do not find much of value in these courses. Reform of music teacher education must take up reform of the methods courses. Leonhard sounded his theme of reconciliation of theory and practice once again, and he reiterated his call for objectives,

[34]Charles Leonhard, Memorandum to Persons Attending the San Antonio Meeting on the Council on Music Teacher Education, n.d. [c. 15 October 1982], original in possession of the author.

[35]Reports from the meetings comprise the entire spring 1985 issue of *Dialogue in Instrumental Music Education*, including an address by Leonhard, a report on the proceedings by Anthony L. Barresi, and a bibliography of research and literature on music teacher education by Thompson Brandt.

modelling, motivating, and evaluating. He urged music teacher educators to provide laboratory experiences or field work experiences for their students in methods courses.[36]

As the time of his retirement approached, Leonhard was, if anything, busier than ever addressing audiences in print and in person in a variety of venues. At this point in his life, he was looking more forward than backward. He was concerned about the future of the profession and consequently attended events and participated in activities that had potential to deal with oncoming issues. While drawing on experiences from many years in the field, he saw the future as more important than the past.

Other leaders in the profession saw the future as an important concern as well. Donald Shetler, for many years the Professor of Music Education at the Eastman School in Rochester, New York, helped organize a conference in conjunction with the Music Educators National Conference in tribute to Howard Hanson. For four days, July 5–8, 1983, 140 participants met to hear papers on the arts in general and on music and music education in particular.[37]

Leonhard's contribution to the festivities at Eastman was a paper on "The Future of Musical Education in America: A Pragmatist's View." He defined music education broadly, not limiting it to kindergarten through

[36] Charles Leonhard, "Methods Courses: An Address Presented to the Symposium on Teacher Education, Madison, Wisconsin, October 24, 1984," *Dialogue in Instrumental Music Education* 9 (Spring 1985): 1–13. This also appeared as "Methods Courses in Music Teacher Education," in *Music Education in the United States: Contemporary Issues*, J. Terry Gates, ed. (Tuscaloosa, AL: The University of Alabama Press, 1988), 193–201.

[37] Donald Shetler, ed., *In Memoriam Howard Hanson: The Future of Musical Education in America* (Rochester, NY: Eastman School of Music Press, 1984), *passim*. Leonhard was one of seven principal speakers. Frank S. M. Hodsoll spoke on "Arts Education and the Arts Endowment"; Christopher Lasch presented "The Degradation of Work and the Apotheosis of Art"; Russell P. Getz read a paper on "Music Education in Tomorrow's Schools: A Practical Approach"; Sidney Hodkinson's essay was on "The Phoenix Revisited: An Etude in Musicomythology"; Willard L. Boyd presented on "Music: Basic Education"; and Robert Freeman's remarks were "On the Need for Bridging Music's Islands."

twelfth grades and identified some critical weaknesses. The main weaknesses were the circularity of music programs, the chasm between art music and popular music, and the homogeneity of the college music program. He also noted some problems with the status of music administration, the lack of unity in the music field, the generally depressed state of the general economy, and mounting criticisms of education in general.[38]

As remedies that might make a significant difference, Leonhard proposed that all parties involved recognize the circularity of music programs in public schools and higher education whereupon students from the public schools go on to colleges and universities, and these institutions in turn train teachers for the public schools. He also urged people working in collegiate institutions to help bridge the gap between art music on the one hand, and popular and ethnic music on the other. He suggested that conductors of college performing groups broaden their repertoires and that colleges and universities teach American vernacular music and a wide variety of ethnic music. He recommended that American composers participate more fully in the musical activities of public schools and colleges, and he urged music schools and programs to highlight their unique attributes rather than trying to look as much like each other as possible.[39]

Leonhard saw that the benefits of his proposed changes would include acceptance of the universality and the uniqueness of music and that teachers would be inclined more toward mutual support and cooperation. He thought that his proposals would make music more accessible to greater numbers of people and that music education programs could become, in a word, comprehensive. He

---

[38]Charles Leonhard, "The Future of Musical Education in America: A Pragmatist's View," in *In Memoriam Howard Hanson: The Future of Musical Education in America*, Donald Shetler, ed. (Rochester, NY: Eastman School of Music Press, 1984), 60–63.

[39]Leonhard, "The Future of Musical Education in America," 63–66.

thought that his ideas might bring about better utilization of resources to meet the needs of students in higher education and that colleges and universities might be able to prepare music administrators. Leonhard presented a concept of a simple and affordable music program for public schools and school music that served the needs of adults, including senior citizens. "Finally, we must seek to establish a broad coalition of professional and amateur musicians and other arts practitioners, arts educators in public and private schools, private teachers of music, and individuals and organizations concerned with the arts and arts education, to participate in political and social action at the local, state, and federal levels of government. A Common Cause for the Arts, if you will."[40]

In early 1984, Leonhard sought yet another venue for dissemination if his ideas. He wrote an article addressed to jazz educators challenging them to deliver what they had promised to the profession and to their students. He urged jazz educators to help students experience the richness and diversity of jazz and to help all educators become better acquainted with the repertoire and performance practices of jazz. He encouraged them to share their unique brand of music making with all music students, and to change instrumental music teaching so that it might regularly include improvisation at beginning as well as at advanced levels.[41]

In March of 1984, Leonhard joined with Allen P. Britton and others in a session on historical research in music education at the biennial convention of the Music Educators National Conference in Chicago. Britton spoke on historical research in music education and its place in graduate programs, and Leonhard followed with an exhortation to historians to be more thorough in writing

---

[40]Leonhard, "The Future of Musical Education in America," 68.

[41]Charles Leonhard, "Has Jazz Education Fulfilled Its Promise?" *Jazz Educators Journal* 16 (December–January 1984): 12–13, and 98.

biographies and do research on more recent topics. He also urged institutions to do a better job of preparing doctoral students to write historical dissertations. "If a student purports to write an historical thesis, the program should be shaped from the beginning to develop historical research skills that will enable the student not only to write a decent thesis, but also to make historical research the focus of his professional life."[42]

In the fall of 1984, Leonhard participated in the Alabama Project: Music, Society and Education in America. From September 20 to October 7, 1984, Leonhard led a team on professional methodology which included Merilyn Jones of the University of Alabama, Gretchen Hieronymous Beall of the University of Colorado, Robert Glidden of The Florida State University, William Jones of Minneapolis, Minnesota, and Richard Graham of the University of Georgia.[43]

Leonhard's presentation recalls the language and ideas of James Mursell. He spoke on "The Human Values of Music Education." Beginning, as he had many an article early in his career, Leonhard defined terms, such as professional methodologies, program development, instruction, administration, supervision, and evaluation. "It is my thesis," he said, "that emphasis on human values should pervade all of the processes at every level of the music education program from early childhood through the graduate school."[44] This, of course, meant musical

[42]Charles Leonhard, "Where's the Beef?" *The Bulletin of Historical Research in Music Education* 5 (July 1984): 59.

[43]J. Terry Gates, foreword to *Music Education in the United States: Contemporary Issues* (Tuscaloosa, AL: The University of Alabama Press, 1988), ix–xi.

[44]Charles Leonhard, "The Human Values of Music Education," in *Music Education in the United States: Contemporary Issues*, ed. J. Terry Gates (Tuscaloosa, AL: The University of Alabama Press, 1988), 186.

experience and musical learning focusing on expressive import. These comprise the basics of music education.

Leonhard addressed Alabama music educators more generally in 1985 with an article on another of his favorite themes: the future of American music education. He began on a positive note about the future of music education, despite some present problems, many created by music educators themselves. Surveying all the calls for reform then current, he concluded that aesthetic considerations were the most important ones music educators could be concerned with, but that they must explain music education as aesthetic education in practical, everyday terms that lay audiences could comprehend and respond to in supportive ways.[45]

In an attempt to communicate more effectively with music educators in general, Leonhard spoke in 1985 via cassette recording and accompanying brochure to members of the Music Educators National Conference. As part of a series of "Words of Note," Leonhard responded again to calls for reform then current and offered his ideas about music education as aesthetic education as an appropriate course of action.[46]

From 1976 through 1985, fifty-six doctoral students completed their dissertations under Leonhard's tutelage, thirteen in the year 1979 alone. Topics and problems ranged from status studies and performance practices to creativity and teaching handicapped children; from assessment and urban settings to administration and biography. Under Leonhard's guidance, doctoral students from 1976 to 1985 wrote status studies and analyses of performance practice.

[45]Charles Leonhard, "1984 and Well Beyond: Can We Be Down to Earth and Still Reach for the Stars?" *Ala Breve* [Journal of the Alabama Music Educators Association] (February 1985): 15–17, 25, and 30.

[46]Charles Leonhard, "Music Education—Aesthetic Education in the Real World of the School," cassette recording, Read by Leonhard, Music Educators National Conference, n.d. [1985]; and Charles Leonhard, *Words of Note: A Realistic Rationale for Teaching Music* (Reston, VA: Music Educators National Conference, 1985).

They surveyed music in special education, John Dewey, and choral rehearsal behaviors; they studied the aesthetics of Monroe Beardsley, the psychology of Granville Stanley Hall, and the musical traditions of the Anuak tribe of Southwestern Ethiopia. They assayed a variety of topics having to do with evaluation, instrumental music instruction, bilingual-bicultural education, and various uses of technology. One of his students from Canada even wrote his dissertation in French. (See Appendix    for a complete listing.)

By the end of 1985, it was beginning to become clear that retirement would be a rather hollow phrase for Leonhard. Though he had but another year to meet his classes on a regular basis, he would continue to teach wherever willing learners might gather. If anything, he was preparing for a busier life in "retirement" than he had ever had while "on the job." If retirement was to have little or no meaning for Leonhard, then he must find something to provide the focus for his ongoing work that would keep him actively working in behalf of the profession and keep in contact with students and music teachers. His ideas about aesthetic education as basic education needed a venue, and the Federal Government would provide it. The National Arts Education Research Center would become his occupation in retirement.

# CHAPTER VIII

# ARTS EDUCATION RESEARCH

Leonhard began his eighth decade on the planet with a variety of activities. He wound down his career on the faculty of the University of Illinois and prepared for retirement which came at the end of the summer of 1986. After a brief fling at some other enterprises, he soon took up the cause for research in arts education with an ambitious and expansive project. He met his obligation to see all of his doctoral students through to completion of their dissertations and defenses, though a good number of them were not finished at the time of his retirement. Some of this work continues at this writing.

The time immediately surrounding Leonhard's retirement was hectic, to say the least. He resigned as chair of the Graduate Committee for Music Education at the end of the fall semester of 1985. His intention was for G. David Peters, who succeeded him in that position, to have time to learn the responsibilities while Leonhard was still around to answer questions. He hosted his own retirement party in May of 1986 at the Champaign Country Club, to which he invited friends and colleagues from the University and the surrounding community.[1]

---

[1]Leonhard to Heller, 23 January 1990; and Charles Leonhard, Urbana, IL, to George N. Heller, Lawrence, KS, 29 September 1993, original in possession of the author.

159

Leonhard's final day of teaching came at the end of the summer session in 1986. At that time, a group of graduate students staged a Greco-Roman style ceremony in honor of his retirement. This moved him to make a public statement (somewhat tongue-in-cheek) about his intentions. On that occasion, Leonhard announced to those assembled that he would

(1) work part-time in an uplifting social agency; (2) serve as a downstate representative of the Hemlock Society and/or the American Civil Liberties Union, the Mother Jones Foundation, the Council in Support of Peace in El Salvador, the Southern Poverty Law Center Klan Watch, People for the American Way, Americans for Democratic Action; (3) go to Las Vegas or the Bahamas when I have a yen for blackjack; (4) go to Florida when I have a yen for the horse track or tire of winter; (5) refrain from uttering or writing one word about music education; (6) refrain from darkening the door of the Music Building lest I cast a long shadow; (7) write on topics within my experience (I have been around every block in town three times); (8) enjoy my family, including the cats.[2]

In addition to all this, he vowed to "bring no disadvantage to anyone except those with whom I play poker or blackjack."[3]

In the fall of 1986, Leonhard set about his retirement activities with the same energy and enthusiasm that had characterized his career in college teaching, research, and service. He delivered meals to persons in Champaign and Urbana who were confined to their homes, he drove cancer patients to and from local hospitals for treatments, he participated in the Adult Diversion Program in the Champaign County State's Attorney's Office. He also tried his hand at handicapping horse races in Florida, and toyed with the idea of opening a gun store in Champaign. During the two years of his retirement, the only commitment

[2]Leonhard to Heller, 29 September 1993.

[3]Ibid.

Figure 17

Leonhard at His Desk, Summer 1986*

*Photograph provided by Charles Leonhard.

Leonhard accepted having anything at all to do with music education was to give the keynote address at the Symposium in honor of the Sesquicentennial of Public School Music (1838–1988) which was held at the University of Maryland in College Park.[4]

Leonhard called his speech at the Sesquicentennial Symposium, "The Past, the Present, and Their Portent for the Future." The occasion offered him an interesting opportunity to reflect on his life and the experiences he had been through. It was also a chance for him to place his life and work in the context of the history of music education. Clearly his mentor, James L. Mursell, was the focus of his reflections.[5]

The talk consisted of four sections, or what Leonhard called generations: the post-World War I years (1920–1940), the Mursell years (1940–1960), the post-Mursell years (1960–1980), and the present. He noted the presence of many great leaders in the first era and the dominance of Mursell in the second. He discussed the rise and flowering of the aesthetic education movement in the third era and concluded with a series of challenges to the music educators in attendance at the Symposium. Leonhard was speaking as if he were getting back in the saddle again, and indeed, he would be returning to work at the University of Illinois within a matter of weeks.[6]

The following year, Leonhard spoke on professional topics again at the University of Toronto and at the National Art Education Association meetings in Kansas City, Missouri. In 1990, he spoke at the University of Maryland,

---

[4]Leonhard to Heller, 29 September 1993.

[5]Charles Leonhard, "The Past, The Present, and Their Portent for the Future," paper presented at the Symposium in Honor of the Sesquicentennial of Public School Music (1838–1938), The University of Maryland, College Park, Maryland, 27 August, 1988.

[6]Ibid.

the University of Cincinnati, Baylor University, and Teachers College, Columbia University. His remarks at Teachers College were in connection with his receiving the Distinguished Alumni Award.[7]

Leonhard spent a good deal of time just prior to his retirement and immediately afterward, giving interviews concerning his life and work. In 1988, he made a significant contribution of his personal papers to Baylor University in Waco, Texas. Barbara L. Bennett, who worked on an oral history project with Leonhard from 1985 to 1990, is on the faculty at Baylor, and she helped provide a suitable location for his books, papers, and other items in the Crouch Music Library on the campus. Included in the collection are tapes and transcripts of thirty-two interviews conducted between 1985 and 1990.[8]

In 1990, at the dedication of the collection of his papers at Baylor, Leonhard spoke on "Music and Musical Education: On the Way to the Promised Land." In that speech, he asserted the essentially romantic nature of musicians. His argument was that the enduring effects of music and music education are its effects on the lives of students, that is, the human values of imagination, feeling, reflection. "The primary role of the music program is to stimulate feelingful thought and thoughtful feeling."[9]

Despite his best efforts to find a life for himself away from music education and away from the University of Illinois, it simply was not to be. In September of 1988, Leonhard returned to the campus as Director of Research for The National Arts Education Research Center, and in

[7]Charles Leonhard, Urbana, IL, to George N. Heller, Lawrence, KS, 10 February 1993, original in possession of the author.

[8]Bennett, "Guide to the Charles Leonhard Special Collection in Music Education"; Bennett, "The Leonhard Connection"; and Bennett, "The Charles Leonhard Oral History Memoirs."

[9]Charles Leonhard, "Music and Musical Education: On the Way to the Promised Land," Paper presented at Baylor University, 10 March 1990.

September 1989, Richard J. Colwell, left the faculty at the University of Illinois to join the faculty at the University of Northern Colorado in Greeley. At that time, Don V. Moses, Director of the School of Music, asked Leonhard to rejoin the Illinois faculty. His primary duties as a member of the faculty were to advise and direct the research of doctoral students in music education. He has remained on the faculty since that time.[10]

As he resumed his place in academia, Leonhard's thoughts turned once again to addressing graduate students in music education. In a speech to the graduate students at the University of Cincinnati in April of 1990, he made a light-hearted attempt to draw parallels between music education in Ancient Greece and the contemporary practice of the profession in the United States. Leonhard used the occasion to call attention to some of the threats to music education which declined markedly in Greece and which is in danger of decline today. As an antidote, he prescribed increased attention to ethnic music, urban and popular music, and musical literacy. Music education must change or face being forced out of the curriculum.[11]

Music teacher education is critical in promoting the needed changes. Leonhard felt that music teachers must "live in the musical and societal present and look to the future rather than seeking to perpetuate the past."[12] Music teacher preparation must produce teachers who not only perform well, but who also know and can work with music history, music criticism, and aesthetics.

Leonhard resumed his professional writing in the Summer of 1990, with an article describing the work of The

[10]Leonhard to Heller, 29 September 1993.

[11]Charles Leonhard, "Can We Continue to Teach the Lyre?" Paper presented at the Graduate Music Education Forum, University of Cincinnati, Cincinnati, OH, 29 April 1990.

[12]Ibid.

National Arts Education Research Center. The article identifies him as Professor Emeritus of Music and Director of Research of The National Arts Education Research Center, University of Illinois at Urbana-Champaign, Urbana, Illinois. In this article, Leonhard explained the genesis of the Center and the activities of its first year (October 1, 1987–September 20, 1988) and its second and third years. He then briefly described the seven projects of the Center.[13]

In a 1991 article on "Aesthetic Literacy in Music," Leonhard compared music education with art education and with drama and theater education. He noted a deficiency in music education concerning music history and criticism. Education, he observed was in a state of theoretical and operational disarray; arts education suffered from chaotic circumstances as well. Music education has seen a complete distortion of the concept of aesthetic education Leonhard began advocating in 1953. He urged educators to accept a simple definition of aesthetic education as education of the senses to respond to expressive import in works of art and to use this definition as a means to the achievement of aesthetic literacy.[14]

Leonhard urged music educators to broaden their conception of music to include not only traditional Western art music, but also American vernacular music and ethnic music from around the world. He offered concrete suggestions for music teaching in elementary, middle, and high schools, and he provided specific recommendations for performing organizations and music teacher education programs. He encouraged music educators to be more open, more creative, and more flexible. "We value right answers

[13]Charles Leonhard, "The National Arts Education Research Center," *Bulletin of the Council for Research in Music Education* 105 (Summer 1990): 1–21.

[14]Charles Leonhard, "Aesthetic Literacy in Music," *Design for Arts in Education* 92 (September-October 1991): 27–29.

from students; we should be teaching them to ask the right questions with regard to all aspects of music and music making. Therein lies the road to aesthetic literacy."[15]

Quite recently, Leonhard was the principal writer of a proposal to incorporate the arts and technology in a community-based school. He and his colleagues submitted their proposal to the New American Schools Development Corporation. It did not gain funding. The proposal takes the position that the arts should be at the core of the curriculum in public schools because of their unique ability to illuminate the other subjects. Involvement of the latest technological tools in this endeavor would help students engage in critical thinking. Emphasizing the arts of diverse ethnic and racial groups would enrich the lives of all students. Involvement of community resources would make the educational program an integral part of the community. The content of the proposal encompassed the thinking of members of a committee organized by Kathryn A. Martin, Dean of the College of Fine and Applied Arts at the University of Illinois. Membership of the committee consisted of representatives from the University of Illinois, New York University, Northern Illinois University, the Kennedy Center for the Performing Arts, the Illinois Alliance for Arts Education, the Getty Foundation, Urban Gateways, Young Audiences, and Opera America.[16]

The major focus of Leonhard's work in the years since 1988 has been with the Illinois site of the National Arts

---

[15]Leonhard, "Aesthetic Literacy in Music," 32.

[16]*The Arts and Technology in a Community-Based School: A Design for Excellence in Education*, a proposal to the New American Schools Development Corporation from the University of Illinois at Urbana-Champaign and the Illinois Alliance for Arts Education, with the cooperation of the Kennedy Center for the Performing Arts (Urbana, IL College of Fine and Applied Arts, University of Illinois, n. d. [1993]). See also, Leonhard to Heller, 10 February 1993; and Charles Leonhard, Urbana, IL, to George N. Heller, Lawrence, KS, 20 October, 1993, original in possession of the author.

Education Research Center in Urbana. He took the position of Director of Research for the Center on October 1, 1988. His work in that position ran through December 1992, when all reports and products of the Center's research and the dissemination effort were completed.[17]

The Center had been under way for a year when Leonhard took the position of Director of Research. He immediately set about clarifying roles of various participants and staff members. One of the major projects for the Center was a survey of arts education in the public schools which Leonhard took charge of. Initially one survey had been planned for education in art, dance, and drama, with a separate survey of music education. Leonhard combined music with the other arts to make it a truly arts-oriented project.[18]

Two publications reported the results of the survey, provided a summary of it, and presented some conclusions drawn from it. The 270-page report gives information gleaned from the thirty-nine item questionnaire sent to a random sample of 1,326 large and small public elementary, middle, and secondary schools across the nation on general characteristics, music, visual art, dance, and drama. The Center mailed the surveys in September of 1989. Sixty-four percent of the schools returned the completed questionnaires.[19]

The format of the report is a series of chapters on music, art, dance, and drama for small elementary schools (fewer than 550 students), large elementary schools (more

[17]Leonhard to Heller, 17 July 1989; and Leonhard, "The National Arts Education Research Center," 4–5.

[18]Leonhard, "The National Arts Education Research Center," 4–5; Leonhard to Heller, 29 September 1993; and Leonhard to Heller, 20 October 1993.

[19]Charles Leonhard, *The Status of Arts Education in American Public Schools* (Urbana, IL: Council for Research in Music Education, 1991), iii–vi.

than 550 students), small middle schools (fewer that 500 students), large middle schools (500 or more students), small secondary schools (smaller than one thousand students), and large secondary schools (one thousand or more students).  Each chapter gives data on student enrollment, ethnic make-up of the student body, parental support for arts education, financial support for arts education, and arts education enrichment activities, as well as detailed information on music, art, dance, and drama at each level.[20]

In summarizing the survey, Leonhard compared it with a similar study of music and art education undertaken in 1962 by the National Education Association.  He found a mixture of positive and negative developments over the twenty-seven years that had intervened between the NEA study and his own.  His general conclusions were that all the arts needed specialist teachers, that music educators needed to teach more than just performance classes (band, choir, and orchestra), that Discipline Based Art Education was a significant movement, that dance and drama programs were gaining ground, that elementary school administrators were allotting too little time for the arts, and that the arts needed increased funding.  Leonhard noted the success arts educators have had in the past, but he urged them to take steps to deal with  educational reform and increasing ethnic and racial diversity in the student population.[21]

Other products of the Center included a monograph by Harry S. Broudy on the role of music in general education, and a collection of essays edited by Ralph A. Smith on the

[20]Leonhard, *The Status of Arts Education*, 1–172.

[21]Charles Leonhard, *The Status of Arts Education: Summary and Conclusions* (Urbana, IL:  Council for Research in Music Education, 1991), 1–45.  Elliot Eisner reviewed  Leonhard's survey in a rather perfunctory manner, describing its contents and format and lamenting that more interpretation and context was not included in the report.  See Elliot W. Eisner, "Two Portraits of Arts Education:  Homegrown in the Midwest," *Educational Researcher* 22 (January–February 1993): 32–34.

arts and cultural literacy. Robert Stake, Liora Bresler, and Linda Mabry used qualitative assessment techniques in their investigation of the arts in elementary schools which resulted in another publication by the Center. G. David Peters developed computerized measures of musical abilities resulting in a publication, computer program, and manual. Dance education accounted for another publication, and the Center published a curriculum guide for drama education. Two other publications in dance education rounded out the work of the Center under Leonhard's direction.[22]

The Center was to have completed its work in December of 1992, but Kathryn A. Martin, Dean of the University of Illinois College of Fine and Applied Arts saw an opportunity to utilize Leonhard's talents and capitalize on his energetic dedication to arts education and vast organizational experience. She has recently directed that the Center continue as a division within the College under the joint leadership of Leonhard and Peters.[23]

As part of his responsibilities with the Center, Leonhard has participated in and supervised dissemination work at conferences and symposia and has participated in several of its other activities. Two of these dissemination

[22]Harry S. Broudy, *The Role of Music in General Music* (Urbana, IL: University of Illinois Press, 1990); Ralph A. Smith, ed. *Cultural Literacy and Arts Education*, special issue of the *Journal of Aesthetic Education* 24 (Spring 1990); Robert Stake, Liora Bresler, and Linda Mabry, *Custom and Cherishing: The Arts in Elementary Schools* (Urbana, IL: Council for Research in Music Education, 1991); G. David Peters, *Musical Skills: A Computer-Based Assessment* (Urbana, IL: Council for Research in Music Education, 1991); Lin Wright, ed., *The Arizona State University K-6 Drama Theatre Curriculum Guide* (Urbana, IL: Council for Research in Music Education, 1991); Patricia Knowles, *Dance Education in American Schools: Case Studies* (Urbana, IL: Council for Research in Music Education, 1991); Patricia Knowles, *Annotated Directory for Dance Education* (Reston, VA: National Dance Association, 1991); and Barbara Magee, *Guidelines for the Development of Documents Addressing K-12 Dance Education Programs* (Urbana, IL: Dance Department, University of Illinois, 1991).

[23]"National Arts Education Research Center—UIUC," brochure, National Arts Education Research Center, Urbana, IL, n.d. [1993]; and Peters, "National Arts Education Research Center."

Figure 18

Leadership of the National Arts Education Research Center*

*Left to right: Kathryn A. Martin, Dean of the College of Fine and Applied Arts; G. David Peters (standing); and Leonhard. Photograph taken from a brochure announcing the National Arts Education Research Center at the University of Illinois.

conferences took place in 1992, one at Annapolis, Maryland in April, and the other at Urbana, Illinois in October.

For the Annapolis Conference, Leonhard offered a paper on "The Status of Arts Education in American Public Schools." This was in large part a summary of his survey, but it also included some new material on arts education requirements for high school graduation and the impact of the recession. He also wrote on the impact of increased academic requirements and discipline-based arts education.[24]

In another document for the Annapolis conference, Leonhard made a proposal for what he thought research in arts education ought to be concerned with. In this proposal, he noted the tradition of arts educators to justify their work for its intrinsic value and for its contributions to other values outside the arts, what John Dewey termed "instrumental values" or others have called "ancillary values." Leonhard made the observation that instrumental values provided much of the rationale for arts education in the nineteenth and early twentieth centuries, but that the idea of aesthetic education had come to the fore in the 1950s and 1960s. Ample funding had afforded arts educators the luxury of justifying their work on intrinsic values. With the movement back to the so-called basics which characterized educational reform in the 1970s and 1980s, Leonhard felt that arts educators would do well to investigate the relationships between studying the arts and performing well in other subjects,

---

[24]Charles Leonhard, "The Status of Arts Education in American Public Schools," paper commissioned for the Symposium on The Arts in American Schools: Setting a Research Agenda for the 1990s, Annapolis, MD, 17–20 May 1992. The National Endowment for the Arts, Arts in Education Program and the U. S. Department of Education, Office of Educational Research and Improvement, Office of Research jointly sponsored this two-day conference. Leonhard's paper was one of several sent to participants in advance of the meetings.

especially language arts, mathematics, history, science, and geography.[25]

Leonhard, along with Kathryn Martin and Theodore Zernich, organized a symposium on "The Future of Arts Education: Arts Teacher Education" at the University of Illinois on October 8–9, 1992. The Symposium was in partial fulfillment of the Center's dissemination responsibilities under the initial grant. Leonhard opened the Symposium with a "Challenge" to the participants. Other project directors also presented papers, and then leaders from each of the four arts education fields addressed the need for and feasibility of changes in teacher education in their areas.[26]

In his challenge, Leonhard expanded on the summary and conclusions from his survey, especially the concerns he had voiced about educational reform and ethnic and racial diversity of students in the public schools. He also noted the increasing demands for cultural literacy and critical thinking, the change in contemporary art styles, and contemporary developments in educational technology. Despite these difficult problems, Leonhard noted the existence of a positive climate for arts education. He challenged participants at the Symposium to work for radical changes in arts teacher preparation "to produce elementary school arts educators who have sufficient understanding and proficiency in all four arts to not only introduce children to those arts but also to serve as resource persons to classroom teachers in relating all of the arts to other subjects in the curriculum."[27]

[25]Charles Leonhard, "A Proposal for Research in Arts Education," remarks made at the Symposium on the Arts in American Schools: Setting a Research Agency for the 1990s," Annapolis, MD, 18 May, 1992.

[26]"The Future of Arts Education: Arts Teacher Education," program, National Arts Education Research Center and The College of Fine and Applied Arts, The University of Illinois at Urbana, Champaign, 1992.

[27]Charles Leonhard, "The Challenge," *Bulletin of the Council for Research in Music Education* 117 (Summer 1993): 1–8.

Late in 1993, the National Arts Education Research Center at the University of Illinois is alive and well under its new auspices. Leonhard continues as Research Director, and David Peters is Administrative Director. Activities currently under way at the Center include faculty proposals for arts assessment, curriculum development, and technology applications. Leonhard and his colleagues are considering a number of projects to advance the ideas of closer linkage among the arts and others which deal with issues such as technology and ethnic and racial diversity.[28]

Although Leonhard taught his last class as a member of the Illinois faculty in the summer session of 1986, he has continued, after a two-year hiatus in 1986–87, to instruct students in individual study, direct research, and advise doctoral dissertations. From 1986 through 1993, twenty-two students have completed doctoral dissertations under Leonhard's supervision.

Leonhard's most recent students have continued a tradition established by their predecessors over the past forty years by pursuing a wide variety of topics. Since 1986, Leonhard's students have written on such topics as high school band teaching and administration, music in higher education, analysis of music literature, biographies of music educators, jazz education, Orff-Schulwerk, music education research literature, children's song literature, computer-based instruction in music, score study and error detection, conductor behavior, and musical theater education. (See Appendix A.)

A perusal of doctoral dissertations completed under Leonhard's supervision reveals the enduring gratitude, nay endearment, of his students. In the "acknowledgements"

[28]G. David Peters, "National Arts Education Research Center: An Overview and Futureview," paper presented at the Symposium on Educational Leadership in the Arts: Music as Art, Science and Entertainment, University of North Carolina at Chapel Hill, 25 September 1993.

section of a recent dissertation, one student thanked him for "His sage advice, clear thinking, inspiration, quick evaluation of submitted materials, prodding, and persistent calls [which] made the completion of this study possible."[29] Another wrote words of heart-felt gratitude to Leonhard for "his support of my career as a musician and educator. His insight as an advisor and his dedication as a teacher are traits for which I have tremendous respect and admiration."[30] Many others echo these same comments with thanks for Leonhard's inspiration, insight, tireless attention, and leadership in supervising their doctoral dissertation research. Virtually without exception, Leonhard's doctoral students give him much of the credit for the inspiration to begin their work and the tenacity to complete it.

Leonhard's work in music education continues unabated. He continues to speak and write on professional topics, he is heavily involved in the National Arts Education Research Center, and he continues to work with doctoral students who are completing their dissertations.

The good company of family and friends is a point of personal pride and a continuing source of enjoyment for Leonhard. His daughter Alicia took her baccalaureate degree at Sophie Newcomb College in New Orleans and her master's at the University of Illinois. She has also earned a master's degree in business administration and a juris doctor degree at the University of Hawaii. She currently lives in Honolulu, where she is an attorney and clerk for a justice of the Hawaii Supreme Court.[31]

[29]Raymond J. Fry, "Development and Trial of a Computer Based Interactive Videodisc Program in a Course in Fundamentals of Conducting" (Ed.D. diss., University of Illinois, 1991), iv.

[30]Thomas F. Birkner, "An Analysis and Classification of Conductor Vocal Communication in the Rehearsals of Selected Jazz Ensembles" (Ed.D. diss., University of Illinois, 1992), iii.

[31]Charles Leonhard, Urbana, IL, to George N. Heller, Lawrence, KS, 6 October 1993, original in possession of the author.

Leonhard's son Chase attended MacMurray College in Jacksonville, Illinois, and he took his bachelor's degree at the University of Illinois. Chase earned the juris doctor degree at Tulane University. He worked for a time as an attorney and as a prosecutor in the Champaign County State Attorney's Office. He currently serves as a member of the Champaign (Illinois) Police Department.[32]

In 1985, Leonhard's wife Patricia retired from a position she held for many years at the University of Illinois: Coordinator of Undergraduate Instruction in the Department of Educational Psychology. She continues her thirty-two year association with the Champaign Park District as a member of its Board of Commissioners.[33]

Leonhard maintains a routine, almost a ritual, that has provided him with much diversion and enjoyment over the past four decades or more. He works the *New York Times* Crossword Puzzle every morning, almost without fail. Once a week, he plays poker with a group of men which has been in existence for thirty-five years. Leonhard is a charter member of the group and he is the only one who still plays regularly. By his own account, Leonhard still "maintains his interest and skill in handicapping horse races."[34]

---

[32]Leonhard to Heller, 6 October 1993.

[33]Ibid.

[34]Ibid.

# EPILOGUE

# CODA BUT NOT FINALE

Leonhard's life has progressed through four stages: youth (1915–1936), rising adulthood (1937–1958), midlife (1959–1980), and retirement (or elderhood, as Howe and Strauss call it, 1981 to the present). In each age and stage of his life, he has approached the problems at hand in his own unique way. In the process he has left an indelible mark on the history of American music education, like other members of his generation, who have left major imprints on America's important institutions. And like other members of his generation, he is filled with hubris, reliant on rationality, and committed to group action.[1]

In reflecting on his life and works, Leonhard says that he feels neither remorse nor despair. "It has really been a great life, and the nice thing is that I come to this time in life with no regrets and no guilt even though most people having done many of the things I have done would spend their declining years saying Pater Nosters and Hail Mary's."[2]

Leonhard's upbringing in Oklahoma was very close to being on the last frontier of American history in both time and place. Anadarko had been settled but a few years when

---

[1]Howe and Strauss, *Generations*, 60–61. In their scheme of ages and stages, Howe and Strauss see the central role of youth (birth to age 21) as dependence, whereas in rising adulthood (ages 22–43) it is activity. In midlife (ages 44–65), the main role is leadership, and in "elderhood" (ages 66–87) it is stewardship. It is not clear what comes after elderhood.

[2]Leonhard to Heller, 1 January 1989.

176

his family lived there, and he spent much of his youth in a dry and dusty corner of the world. That world would soon undergo radical changes. Whatever hardships his mother and father had to endure, and there were many, they saw to it that their children not only had a basic education, but also piano lessons, trips to concerts and contests, and many other cultural experiences that parents of today often find neither the time nor the resources to provide.

Leonhard acknowledges some of the shortcomings and failings of his life, but does so with equanimity and with gratitude for what has been enjoyable. "Everybody should live such a life as I have had. It has been colorful, varied, and dramatic in many respects; while it has by no means been blameless, the nice thing about it is that I have never had any sense of guilt and look back on it with almost no regret. Rue does not apply even to the gamier events and experiences, of which there have been many."[3]

In college at the University of Oklahoma, in his public school teaching, and in other experiences of his early adulthood, Leonhard came into contact with music and other cultural activities from a world well beyond the Oklahoma borders. While his parents and others of their generation may have been weighted down with the aftermath of World War I and the onset of the Great Depression, Leonhard and his youthful colleagues seem to have been inspired by the challenges of that difficult time. Something of a loner in his youth, still he studied with people who had been trained in New York City and in other centers of music and art, and he developed a longing to experience these cultural meccas for himself.

The Second World War was a crystallizing experience for Leonhard as it was for many people his age. Here the youthful optimism persisted and resulted in action once

[3]Charles Leonhard, Urbana, IL, to Bruce D. Wilson, College Park, MD, 26 January 1989, photocopy in possession of the author.

again. Here he learned to face real, life-threatening danger and to test his mettle, largely among his peers. In the South Pacific, Leonhard learned to take on responsibility. He experienced excitement on a grand scale, and he participated in the triumph of the century. The whole experience was, in a word, heroic.

After the war, Leonhard set about realizing his dreams. With his war experience, his back pay, and the possibility of getting funds through the G. I. Bill if needed, he went to New York. There he taught on a fellowship and studied with the likes of Julius Herford, Susanne K. Langer, James L. Mursell, and many others who were in the vanguard of aesthetics, music, and music education at that time. He even touched base with giants from the previous era, John Dewey and Peter W. Dykema, who were then in the twilight of their careers at Teachers College.

On the faculty in music education at the University of Illinois for the past forty-two years, Leonhard has put into practice the things he spent a lifetime acquiring. It was in this position that he taught so many doctoral students and edited a general music series and a series of books on music education. It was at Illinois that Leonhard developed his approach to music and music education that made him noteworthy in the field. It was at Illinois that Leonhard made aesthetic education a byword in the profession. Illinois was where people came to study and to learn about the ideas that Leonhard first introduced to them.

As a colleague, both at the University and in the profession, Leonhard was very selective. He developed a small circle of friends, people whom he respected and got along well with. Allen Britton first got to know Leonhard in 1952. The two men got along well from the outset and have remained good friends for over forty years. "Charlie," Britton recalled, "seemed to be the perfect embodiment of the sophisticated New Yorker. I saw no pretense in him. Besides, he was knowledgeable about Susanne Langer. That impressed me, because at the time [Langer] was not an object of attention in music education."[4]

Many people in music education identify the term aesthetic education with Leonhard and with the University of Illinois. Leonhard's work with Susanne Langer at Teachers College and his formulation of the idea of building a graduate program in music education around the concept of aesthetic education are certainly important contributions. His lifelong efforts to publish articles in many and diverse professional publications and to speak countless times before all kinds of audiences about his ideas have strengthened the identification of Leonhard with aesthetic education. The fact that he is a gifted writer and a striking speaker has also helped spread the word of aesthetic education, to evangelize, as it were.

Leonhard's relationship with the Music Educators National Conference is an interesting puzzle. In his early adulthood, while studying at Teachers College, he seems to have been very interested in participating in the organization. This was largely a result of constructive working relationships he had with one-time MENC president, Lilla Belle Pitts, and her good friend Vanett Lawler, who was then the MENC Executive Secretary.

When he first went to Illinois, Leonhard soon became involved with the MENC-sponsored *Journal of Research in Music Education*, and later he served on the Editorial Committee of the *Music Educators Journal* from 1968 to 1972. Since then, he has had relatively little to do with the MENC. At times, he has even been rather outspoken in his criticism of the organization and of some of the people who held leadership roles in it. Nevertheless, he frequently wrote

[4]Britton to Heller, 18 February 1989.

for the *Music Educators Journal* and was the founder of the
MENC Society for Music Teacher Education in 1982. The
Society continues to grow and develop as a positive force for
the reform of music teacher education.[5]

Britton, who had himself served as President of the
MENC and had invited Leonhard to be on the initial Editorial
Committee of the *JRME*, commented that "Charlie is in some
ways a kind of loner who tends to have a poor opinion of the
workings of big organizations like the MENC and, I think it
fair to say, also of many individual laborers in the
educational vineyard. In spite of the fact that he always
seemed to include me within a kind of favored circle of those
few who were not completely incompetent."[6]

Retirement has been a difficult time in Leonhard's life.
He had tried very hard to prepare himself intellectually for
the experience, but things simply did not go the way he had
planned. He tried to wrap up his career at Illinois and in the
profession with some concluding activities, but they
somehow did not seem to work, or people responded to
them in ways he did not anticipate.

In 1984, when Leonhard thought his career was
coming to an end, he went to the MENC convention in
Chicago and while there hosted his final get-together for
Illinois graduates and, in general bade farewell to friends and
colleagues in the profession, and to his former students.
Britton recalled that on that occasion Leonhard "said that he
never would make another speech, that he was not going to
go 'nattering in senility' before the eyes of his colleagues."
After the speech, Britton "went up to congratulate him on his
speech, which was stimulating as always, and without
giving it much forethought, put out my hand and said,

[5]Eunice L. Boardman, "Society for Music Teacher Education: The
Formative Years," *Journal of Music Teacher Education* 1 (Spring 1992):
2–4.

[6]Britton to Heller, 18 February 1989.

'Goodbye forever, Charlie.' I think he flinched, just a little."[7]

Since his brief period of retirement, it has become clear that Leonhard still has much to contribute, both to students at the University of Illinois and to the profession at large. His return to the University of Illinois and his involvement with the National Arts Education Research Center provide him with ideal opportunities to continue his work in a meaningful way. It will be interesting to see what becomes of this project as Leonhard and his colleagues work to promote the idea of a unified approach to arts education after a fashion not now commonly accepted in most schools, colleges, and universities.

Leonhard's personality is interesting, if somewhat enigmatic, for a biographer to study. He claims to have had an inhibited youth, filled with solitude and shyness. In later years, he acquired a reputation for forwardness, which he claims is a cover for his fundamentally reticent nature. He admits to some flamboyant habits, such as playing cards and wagering on horses. His participation in these activities has contributed to a somewhat swashbuckling image that friends and colleagues have of him.[8]

Britton commented that "While I was chairman of the music ed department [at The University of Michigan], I used to invite Charlie here [to Ann Arbor] for summer sessions. He always delighted everybody, and he told me that he was delighted to come, not only to get out of the heat in Urbana, but because of the close proximity of the famous Michigan race track."[9] Leonhard taught at Michigan for two summer

---

[7]Britton to Heller, 18 February 1989.

[8]Boardman interview.

[9]Britton to Heller, 18 February 1989.

sessions in the 1960s, and he did indeed frequent the Detroit Race Course on those occasions.[10]

> I guess that Charlie is what we call a character.  His intelligence, verve, and personality have enabled him to exert a tremendous influence on the course of music education in this country, all for the good.  You can see it in the content of the general music series, and in the much improved intellectualizing of the profession.  His students are loyal to him and to his ideas.  You know who they are.[11]

Indeed, as one reads through the dedication pages of the nearly two hundred doctoral dissertations for which Leonhard was either the principal advisor or a member of the advisory committee, the awe in which his students hold him comes through clearly.  They give him effusive praise for stimulating their thinking, and they write of how he inspired them to realize previously unknown abilities.  As they go out into the world and make successes of themselves, some occasionally write back a word of thanks.  They write of how their contact with him opened their eyes to their own inner strengths.  They write of how he introduced them to the importance of philosophy in teaching music.  They write of how he left his mark on them as musicians and as human beings.  No doubt there are those who see Leonhard in a lesser light.  They, of course, do not write him letters, nor do they share their feelings publicly to any great extent.  On the contrary, countless students have written to Leonhard over the years expressing their gratitude.[12]

Leonhard constantly reminded his students about the need to involve their own students directly in real and

[10]Leonhard to Heller, 25 August 1993.

[11]Britton to Heller, 18 February 1989.

[12]One recent example is from Donna Dinsmore, Spartanburg, SC, to Charles Leonhard, Urbana, IL, 24 November 1993, photocopy in possession of the author.

genuine musical experiences. He argued along with John Dewey that music educators must work for continuity between art and experience. He advocated this not only for students in public schools, but for all people. As the years passed and as life became increasingly complicated by technology and cultural diversity and countless other factors, he held to this idea ever more firmly.[13]

Leonhard's contributions to the profession, both in his own work and in that of his students, have left a major mark and continue unabated. His early work on evaluation, philosophy, and general music, as well as his contributions to other areas is significant and lasting. His ideas about music education as aesthetic education are still very important. It is impossible to measure his effect on the thousands of public school children who grew up singing songs from the Discovering Music Together series and listening to its recordings. No one can begin to measure the impact of his efforts and ideas on thousands of students and teachers who have read *Foundations and Principles of Music Education* or any of the several books in the Prentice-Hall series which he edited. It seems safe to conclude that it must be momentous.

Music teachers no longer depend entirely on "Dance Macabre" when explaining what music is supposed to mean to seventh graders. Charlie has always been in the vanguard of those who teach music as music, without regard to currently popular educational fads.[14]

[13] Charles Leonhard, "People's Art Programs: A New Context for Music Education," *Music Educators Journal* 66 (April 1980): 36–39; reprinted in *The Music Educator and Community Music*, ed. Michael L. Mark (Reston, VA: Music Educators National Conference, 1992), 29–33.

[14] Britton to Heller, 18 February 1989.

# APPENDIX

## LEONHARD DOCTORAL DISSERTATION ADVISEES

During his tenure at the University of Illinois, Charles Leonhard advised 177 doctoral dissertations. He arrived at Illinois in 1951, when the doctoral program was relatively new. The first of his graduates finished in 1954, and for the next forty-one years, students completed their work under his tutelage at the rate of well over four per year.

| | | | | |
|---|---|---|---|---|
| 1954 | 2 | | 1964 | 8 |
| 1955 | 2 | | 1965 | 4 |
| 1956 | 1 | | 1966 | 3 |
| 1957 | 3 | | 1967 | 5 |
| 1958 | 4 | | 1968 | 3 |
| 1954–58 | 12 | | 1964–68 | 23 |
| | | | | |
| 1959 | 0 | | 1969 | 6 |
| 1960 | 5 | | 1970 | 5 |
| 1961 | 6 | | 1971 | 6 |
| 1962 | 4 | | 1972 | 8 |
| 1963 | 7 | | 1973 | 8 |
| 1959–63 | 22 | | 1969–73 | 33 |

| | | | |
|---|---|---|---|
| 1974 | 4 | 1984 | 4 |
| 1975 | 2 | 1985 | 2 |
| 1976 | 7 | 1986 | 10 |
| 1977 | 8 | 1987 | 0 |
| 1978 | 6 | 1988 | 0 |
| 1974–78 | 27 | 1984–88 | 16 |
| 1979 | 13 | 1989 | 0 |
| 1980 | 7 | 1990 | 2 |
| 1981 | 3 | 1991 | 6 |
| 1982 | 6 | 1992 | 4 |
| 1983 | 3 | | |
| 1979–83 | 32 | 1984–93 | 12 |

## 1954

House, Robert W. "A Proposed Curriculum for Preparing Teachers of Music at Kearney State Teachers College."
Shepard, John W. "Principles of Method in Group String Instruction."

## 1955

Cucci, Angelo M. "A Study of Practices and Characteristics in Secondary School Music Education Programs Related to Student Participation in Musical Activities."
Humphreys, Alfred W. "A Follow-Up Study of the Graduates of the School of Music, University of Illinois."

## 1956

Worthington, Richard A. "An Analysis of Doctoral Theses in Music Education, 1940–1954."

## 1957

Blyler, Dorothea May. "The Song Choices of Children in the Elementary School."
Thomas, Robert E. "A Report on Music Supervision in the Elementary Schools of Champaign, Illinois, 1954-57."
Worrel, J. William. "An Evaluation of Teacher Preparation in Music Education at the University of Kentucky Through an Analysis of the Opinions of Graduates."

## 1958

Riggin, Glen W. "Developing Instructional Materials for Beginning Students of Wind Instruments."

Robertson, James H. "Principles for General Music in Secondary Schools."

Watkins, Robert H. "The Construction and Testing of a Forced Choice Scale for the Evaluation of Student Teachers in Vocal Music at the Junior High School Level."

Williams, Raymond E. "The Measurement and Prediction of Cooperating Teacher Effectiveness in Music Teacher Education."

## 1959

No dissertations.

## 1960

Crockett, Frank M., Jr. "An Analysis and Evaluation of the University of Texas Program of String Teacher Preparation."

Grover, Paul B. "The History of String Class Instruction in American Schools and Its Relationship to School Orchestras."

Reynolds, George E. "Environmental Sources of Musical Awakening in Pre-School Children."

Rutan, Harold D. "An Annotated Bibliography of Written Material Pertinent to the Performance of Brass and Percussion Chamber Music."

Squire, Alan P. "An Annotated Bibliography of Written Material Pertinent to the Performance of Woodwind Chamber Music."

## 1961

Colwell, Richard J. "An Investigation of Achievement in Music in the Public Schools of Sioux Falls, South Dakota."

Colwell, Ruth Ann. "The Development of a Theoretical Basis for a Course in Music Appreciation at the College Level."

Duda, Walter B. "The Prediction of Three Major Dimensions of Teacher Behavior for Student Teachers in Music Education."

Garretson, Homer E. "An Annotated Bibliography of Written Material Pertinent to the Performance of Chamber Music for Stringed Instruments."

Gould, A. Oren. "The Flute Sonatas of Georg Friedrich Handel: A Stylistic Analysis and Historical Study."

Smith, Robert B. "A Study of the Effect of Large-Group Vocal Training on the Singing Ability of Nursery School Children."

## 1962

Hoffren, James A. "The Construction and Validation of a Test of Expressive Phrasing in Music."

Mathis, George R. "A Study of Music Teacher Preparation at Illinois Wesleyan University, 1930–1959."

Pence, John R. "Theoretical Considerations and Illustrative Approaches in Professional Education Methods Courses for Teachers of Music."

Simmons, Donald W. "The Motivations and Musical Backgrounds of Participants and Non-Participants in Selected Community Choruses."

## 1963

Busche, Henry E. "The History of High School Choral Activities in Three Selected Cities of the United States."

Harrison, Ruthann. "A Program for the Preparation of Choral Directors."

Leonard, Janet M. "Change in Status of Music Education Between 1955 and 1961 in Public Schools of Selected Cities Between 100,000 and 200,000 Population."

Lutz, Warren W. "The Personality Characteristics and Experiential Backgrounds of Successful High School Instrumental Teachers."

Pflederer [Zimmerman], Marilyn. "The Responses of Children to Musical Tasks Embodying Piaget's Principle of Conservation."

Reimer, Bennett. "The Common Dimensions of Aesthetic and Religious Experience."

Weber, Calvin E. "The Contribution of Albert Austin Harding and His Influence on the Development of School and College Bands."

## 1964

Aurand, Wayne O. "An Experimental Study of College Music Methods Class Laboratory School Participation Experience."

Boardman, Eunice L. "An Investigation of the Effect of Preschool Training on the Development of Vocal Accuracy in Young Children."

Estes, William V. "Change in Status of Music Education Between 1955–56 and 1961–62 in Public School Systems of Selected Cities between 50,000 and 100,000 Population."

King, Robert F., Jr. "A Study of Tempo Deviations in Recorded Performances of Selected Symphonies by Haydn and Mozart."

Neice, Thomas E. "An Investigation of the Relationships of Selected Factors in the Preparation of Music Education Majors to Musical Achievement."

Pearman [Sharp], Martha. "A Theoretical Framework with Adaptable Instructional Material for General Music Classes at the Secondary Level."

Schuetz, Warren H. "An Evaluation of the Music Program at the University of Illinois High School."

Smith, Robert C. "Aesthetic Theory and the Appraisal of Practices in Music Education."

## 1965

Labuta, Joseph A. "A Theoretical Basis for College Instrumental Conducting Courses."

Motycka, Arthur. "A Report on the Results of an Experimental Course of Study in General Music."

Sheckler, Lewis R. "Charles Alexander Fullerton: His Life and Contribution to Music Education."

Waa, Loren R. "An Experimental Study of Class and Private Methods of Instruction in Instrumental Music."

## 1966

Brinkman, James M. "The German Male Chorus: Its Role and Significance from 1800-1850."

Johnston, William L. "An Appraisal of Music Programs in the Public Schools of Illinois Excluding Chicago."

Newman, Grant H. "The Effects of Programmed Learning on Achievement and Attitude in a Music Course for Classroom Teachers."

## 1967

Beall, N. Gretchen Hieronymus. "Meaningful Reception Learning and Secondary School General Music."

Maharg, John M. "The Development and Appraisal of a Course in Choral Music."

Slagle, Harold C. "An Investigation of the Effect of Seven Methods of Instruction on the Musical Achievement of Elementary Education Majors."

Townsend, George D. "A Stylistic and Performance Analysis of the Clarinet Music of Paul Hindemith."

Tuley, Robert. "A Study of Musical Achievement of Elementary and Junior High School Pupils at Malcolm Price Laboratory School of the State College of Iowa."

## 1968

Prince, Joe N. "An Evaluation of Graduate Music Education Programs at the University of Illinois."

Rabin, Marvin. "History and Analysis of the Greater Boston Youth Symphony Orchestra from 1958–1964."

Roehmann, Franz L. "A Theoretical Basis for the Teaching of Music Theory to Music Majors at the Undergraduate College Level."

## 1969

Johnson, James R. "The Change in Status of Public School String Programs in Minnesota Between the Schools Years 1959–60 and 1967–68."

Mathie, Gordon W. "A Theoretical Basis for College Trumpet Study."

Shugert, James M. "An Experimental Investigation of Heterogeneous Class and Private Methods of Instruction with Beginning Instrumental Music Students."

Sibbing, Robert V. "An Analytical Study of the Published Sonatas for Saxophone by American Composers."

Williams, Franklin E. "Music Instruction in the Colleges Affiliated with the American Lutheran Church: An Appraisal and Proposed Plan for Improvement."

Williams, Robert E. "A Learning Sequence for Beginners on the Clarinet Based on an Investigation of Musical and Manipulative Difficulties Found in Junior High Band Music."

## 1970

Elrod, Wilburn T. "The Effects of Programmed Instruction on Achievement and Attitude of College Freshman Music Theory Students."

Erickson, Karle J. "The Choral Music of Daniel Moe: A Stylistic and Performance Analysis."

Grose, Gerald K. "A Study of the Effect of Use of the Video Taperecorder in the Teaching of Beginning Conducting."

Hanson, Richard D. "An Analysis of Selected Choral Works of F. Melius Christiansen."

Kudlawiec, Dennis P. "The Application of Schenkerian Concepts of Musical Structure to the Analysis Segment of Basic Theory Courses at the College Level"

## 1971

Bennett, M. Donald. "The Effects of Persuasive Communication, Persuasive Communication with Group Discussion, and Persuasive Communication with Role-Playing on Changing the Attitude of Freshman and Sophomore Music Majors Toward Twelve-Tone Music."

Duckworth, William E. "Expanding Notational Parameters in the Music of John Cage."

Koper, Robert P. "A Stylistic Analysis of the Bassoon Music of Paul Hindemith."

Sorenson, James M. "The Effects of Small Ensemble Experiences on Achievement and Attitude of Selected Junior High School Instrumental Music Students."

Swickard, John H. "A Comparative Study of Music Achievement of Students in Grades Four, Five, and Six."

Tiede, Russell L. "A Study of the Effects of Experience in Evaluating Unidentified Instrumental Performance on the Student Conductor's Critical Perception of Performance."

## 1972

Bates, Duane A. "The Status of Music Education in 1969–70 in the Cities of Southern Ontario Having a Population in Excess of 100,000."

Boone, Dalvin L. "The Treatment of the Trumpet in Six Published Chamber Works Composed Between 1920 and 1929."

Erbes, Robert L. "The Development of an Observation System for the Analysis of Interaction in the Rehearsal of Musical Organizations."

Medlin, Douglas S. "A Critical Review and Synthesis of Doctoral Research in the Methodology of Music Teaching."

Patterson, Lawrence W. A. "Undergraduate Programs for Music Teacher Preparation in Canadian Colleges and Universities."

Piper, Robert N. "An Evaluation of the ACDA *Choral Journal.*"

Placek, Robert W. "Design and Trial of a Computer-Assisted Lesson in Rhythm."

Tromblee, Maxwell R. "An Investigation of the Effectiveness of Programmed Drill Training in Teaching Intonation Discrimination Skills."

## 1973

Brown, Frank W.  "The History of the Corning Philharmonic Orchestra and Its Current Role in Community Music Education in Corning, New York."

Gates, J. Terry.  "A Philosophy of Music Education Based on the Writings of John Dewey."

Knight, George W.  "A Comparative Study of Compositional Techniques Employed in Instructional Materials and Twentieth-Century Solos for the Clarinet."

Olsen, Richard N.  "Howard A. Murphy, Theorist and Teacher:  His Influence on the Teaching of Basic Music Theory in American Colleges and Universities from 1940 to 1973."

Peters, G. David.  "Feasibility of Computer-Assisted Instruction for Instrumental Music Education."

Roller, Dale A.  "The Secular Choral Music of Jean Berger."

Sudano, Gary R.  "Aesthetic Theory:  Its Uses in Music Education."

Welch, Myron D.  "The Life and Work of Leonard Falcone with Emphasis on His Years as Director of Bands at Michigan State University."

## 1974

Cooksey, John M.  "An Application of the Facet-Factorial Approach to Scale Construction in the Development of a Rating Scale for High School Choral Performance."

Leman, John W.  "A Descriptive Study of the Undergraduate Music Education Program for the Preparation of Choral Directors at Five Midwestern Universities During the 1972-73 School Year."

Palmer, Mary H. "The Relative Effectiveness of the Richards and the Gordon Approaches to Rhythm Reading for Fourth Grade Children."

Sullivan, Henry F. "A Descriptive Study of the Musical, Academic, and Social Characteristics of Selected Students in a Suburban High School in New York State."

## 1975

Gerber, Linda L. "An Examination of Three Early Childhood Programs in Relation to Early Childhood Music Education."

Kidd, Robert L., III. "The Construction and Validation of a Scale of Trombone Performance Skills."

## 1976

Corcoran, Gerald J., Jr. "The Current Status of Kansas School Music Programs in Relation to Standards for 'Basic Programs' Established by the Music Educators National Conference."

Fenley, J. Franklin. "The Ornamentation in Seven Flute Sonatas Composed by or Attributed to J. S. Bach."

Gorder, Wayne D. "An Investigation of Divergent Production Abilities as Constructs of Musical Creativity."

Larson, Richard C. "The Relationships Among the Academic, Musical, and Aural Abilities of Fredonia College Music Majors."

Rosene, Paul E. "A Field Study of Wind Instrument Training for Educable Mentally Handicapped Children."

Wessler, Robert A. "An Assessment of Achievement and Attitude Toward Music Education Among Fourth, Fifth, and Sixth Grade Students in Corozal, Puerto Rico."

Woodruff, Benjamin W., Jr. "Rachmaninoff's Orchestral Works: A Descriptive Commentary."

## 1977

Daugherty, Elza L. "The Application of Manhattanville Music Curriculum Strategies in a Music Class for Elementary Music Education Majors."

Harris, Thomas J. "An Investigation of the Effectiveness of an Intonation Training Program upon Junior and Senior High School Wind Instrumentalists."

Hawkins, Garland M. "Urban Secondary General Music Teachers' Opinions of Selected Behavioral and Expressive Objectives."

Key, Roderick E. "Demographic Characteristics and Sources of Motivation of Chief Administrators of Music Departments in American Colleges and Universities."

Reichmuth, Roger E. "Price Doyle, 1896–1967: His Life and Work."

Tenzer, Lawrence R. "The Process of Imagination in John Dewey's Philosophy of Aesthetic Experience."

Thurman, K. Leon. "A Frequency and Time Description of Selected Rehearsal Behaviors Used by Five Choral Conductors."

Winking, John T. "The Application of Monroe Beardsley's Theory of Aesthetics to the Structuring of Music Listening Experiences."


## 1978

Osterlund, David C. "The Anuak Tribe of South Western Ethiopia: A Study of Music within the Context of Its Sociocultural Setting."

Rideout, Roger R. "Granville Stanley Hall and Music Education: 1880–1924."

Schumaker, Ralph B., Jr. "An Evaluation of the Graduate Music Education Programs at East Carolina University."

Williams, Edmund C. "The Use of Videotape in the Solution of Selected Problems in Oboe Playing—A Field Study."

Wing, Lizabeth A. "Formative Evaluation in the Secondary General Music Classroom."

Yoder, Chris. "Theodore Presser, Educator, Publisher, Philanthropist: Selected Contributions to the Music Teaching Profession in America."


## 1979

Burley, John M. "A Feasibility Study of Structured Instruction in Instrumental Music for the Adult Beginner."

Dawley, Robert M. "An Analysis of the Methodological Orientation and the Music Literature Used in the Suzuki Violin Approach."

Diaz, C. Herminio. "A Descriptive Study of Music Programs in Roberto Clemente High School and Selected Feeder Schools as They Relate to Bilingual-Bicultural Education."

Etzel, Sr. Marion. "The Effect of Training Upon Children's Ability in Grades One Through Six to Perform Selected Musical Listening Tasks."

Flohr, John W. "Musical Improvisation Behavior of Young Children."

Grabarski, Sam W. "The Performing Art Center Movement in the United States (Excluding Campus-Related Centers)."

Jordan, George L. "Videotape Supplementary Instruction in Beginning Conducting."

Kelly, Justin M. "The College Voice Class: The Development and Trial of a Behavioral Objectives Approach to Teaching College Voice Classes."

Khoshzamir, Mojtaba. "Ali Naqi Vaziri and His Influence on Music Education in Iran."

Maxwell, David H. "The Effect of Training on the Development of Pitch Identification Ability in Elementary School Children."

Miller, Robert F. "An Analysis of Musical Perception Through Multi-Dimensional Scaling."

Schmitt, Sr. M. Cecilia K. "Development and Validation of a Measure of Self-Esteem of Musical Ability."

Steckman, Harry M. "The Development and Trial of a College Course in Music Literacy Based Upon the Kodály Method."

## 1980

Bowman, Wayne D. "Tacit Knowing, Musical Experience, and Music Instruction: The Significance of Michael Polanyi's Thought for Music Education."

Diaz [Nelson], Margaret C. "An Analysis of the Elementary School Music Series Published in the United States from 1926 to 1976."

Price, Dennis R. "Perceptions of Administrators, Music Supervisors, and Music Teachers in Regard to the Role of Music Supervision in the Commonwealth of Virginia."

Ringuette, Raymond. "Considérations théoriques sur l'organisation et la direction d'un programme de formation de musiciens éducateurs à l'Université Laval" ["A Theoretical Basis of the Music Teacher Education Program at Laval University"] (French Text)

Thomas, Robert F., Jr. "An Evaluation of the Music Education Program at Claflin College."

Tiboris, Peter E. "A Study of the Feasibility of Constructing a Performance Difficulty Assessment Scale for Musical Theater."

Young, Jerry A. "The Tuba in the Symphonic Works of Anton Bruckner and Gustav Mahler: A Performance Analysis."

## 1981

Covington, Victoria L. "Approaches to Piano Reading in a Selected Sample of Current Instructional Materials for Adult Beginners."

O'Neill [Seibel], Mary T. "Music Learning Behaviors at Four Age Levels."

Reese, Sam. "An Implementation of the CEMREL Aesthetic Education Program by Elementary Classroom Teachers: A Qualitative Observation."

## 1982

Akrofi, Eric A. "The Status of Music Education Programs in Ghanaian Public Schools."

Dilley, Allen L. "The Effect of Summer Band Camp Experience on Selected Aspects of Musical Competency."

Gregory, Earle S. "Mark H. Hindsley: The Illinois Years."

Locke, John R. "Influences on the College Choice of Freshman Music Majors in Illinois."

Pontious, Melvin F. "A Profile of Rehearsal Techniques and Interaction of Selected Band Conductors."

Secrest, Joseph D. "Continuing Education in Music: A Study of Successful Practices, Innovative Strategies, and Current Trends."

## 1983

Grant, Joe W., Jr. "Choral Music Education in Five Midwestern Collegiate Institutions."

Hearson, Robert H. "Leadership and Self-Confidence: A Case Study Investigation of the Relationship of Prior Experiences to Self-Confidence, Leadership, and Student Teaching."

Shand, Patricia M. M. "A Guide to Unpublished Canadian String Orchestra Music Suitable for Student Performers."

## 1984

Behmer, Carl F. "The Effect of a Learning Program on the Ability of Undergraduate Music Students to Detect Errors in Performance."

Bingham, John S. "The Innovative Uses of the Trombone in Selected Compositions of Vinko Globokar."

Patterson, Russell S. "Conducting Gestures Used by High School Choral Directors."

Thiel, Cynthia R. "Participant Observation Study of a Fourth Grade Music Classroom.

## 1985

Harris [Dodohara], Jean N. "The Instructional Philosophies Reflected in the Elementary Music Series Published by Silver Burdett Company, 1885–1975."

Magnusdottir, Anna M. "Toward a Phenomenology of Music."

## 1986

Bell, John R. "The High School Band: Instructional Tasks, Administrative Tasks, and Terminal Outcomes."

Dorough, Prince L. "A History of the Montevallo Department of Music, 1918–1984."

Edwards, Lawrence A. "'*Die Gottin im Putzzimmer*,' by Richard Strauss."

Harwood, Eve E. "The Memorized Song Repertoire of Children in Grades Four and Five in Champaign, Illinois."

Johnson, Ronald W. "Wind Ensembles in Six American Collegiate Institutions."

LaRue, Peter J. "A Study to Determine the Degree of Consensus Regarding Outcomes of Band Participation and Competitive Elements in Band Programs among Band Directors, Band Members, and Members of Band Parent Booster Groups."

Latta, John A. "Alice Parker: Composer, Arranger, and Teacher."

Lidral, Karel A. "Four Pieces by James Knapp for Jazz Ensemble: Systematic Analyses and Performance Guidelines."

Munsen, Sylvia C. "A Description and Analysis of an Orff-Schulwerk Program of Music Education."

Stabler, Dennis G. "A Content Analysis of the *Bulletin of the Council for Research in Music Education*, 1963–1985."

1987

No dissertations.

1988

No dissertations.

## 1989

No dissertations.

## 1990

Chong, Sylvia N. Y. "General Music Education in the Primary Schools in Singapore, 1959–1990."

Sigurjónsson, Jón H. "Interaction of College Students with Twentieth-Century Music in a Computer Environment."

## 1991

Atwater, David F. "The Development and Trial of Computer-Based Interactive Videodisc Courseware for Teaching Skills in the Visual Diagnosis of Selected Problems in Trombone Performance."

Chan, Felix C. "The Development of Technique for Playing the Waltzes of Frédéric Chopin."

Drafall, Lynn E. "The Use of Developmental Clinical Supervision with Student Teachers in Secondary Choral Music: Two Case Studies."

Hile, James W. "Harry Begian: On Bands and Band Conducting."

Hopkins, Jesse E. "The Effect of Four Approaches to Score Study on Student Conductors' Ability to Detect Errors in the Performance of Choral Music."

Stroud, Stephen L. "An Examination of Five Active University Band Directors Selected as Exemplary Conductors."

<u>1992</u>

Baker, Katherine M. "Significant Experiences, Influences, and Relationships in the Educational and Professional Development of Three Music Educators: Gretchen Hieronymus Beall, Eunice Louise Boardman, and Mary Henderson Palmer."

Birkner, Thomas, F. "An Analysis and Classification of Conductor Vocal Communication in the Rehearsals of Selected Jazz Ensembles."

Foust, Diane, "Musical Theatre Education: A Case Study."

Fry, Raymond J. "Development and Trial of a Computer-Based Interactive Videodisc Program in a Course in Fundamentals of Conducting."

# BIBLIOGRAPHY

## Books and Pamphlets

Andrews, Frances M. *Junior High General Music.* Englewood Cliffs, NJ: Prentice-Hall, Inc., 1971.

Broudy, Harry S. *The Role of Music in General Music.* Urbana, IL: University of Illinois Press, 1990

Brownell, Clifford Lee, and E. Patricia Hagman. *Physical Education—Foundations and Principles.* New York: McGraw-Hill Book Company, Inc., 1951.

Colwell, Richard J., ed. *Basic Concepts in Music Education II.* Niwot, CO: University Press of Colorado, 1991.

_____. *Symposium in Music Education: A Festchrift for Charles Leonhard.* Urbana, IL: University of Illinois, 1982.

Costello, John. *The Pacific War.* New York: Rawson, Wade, 1981.

Cremin, Lawrence A. *American Education: The Metropolitan Experience, 1876–1980.* New York: Harper & Row Publishers, Inc, 1988.

Gibson, Arrell Morgan. *Oklahoma: A History of Five Centuries.* 2nd ed. Norman, OK: University of Oklahoma Press, 1981.

Gittinger, Roy. *The University of Oklahoma, 1892–1942.* Norman, OK: University of Oklahoma, 1942.

Green, Elizabeth A. H. *Teaching Stringed Instruments in Classes.* Englewood Cliffs, NJ: Prentice-Hall, Inc., 1966.

Hagman, E. Patricia. *Good Health for You and Your Family*. New York: A. S. Barnes, 1951.

Heller, George N. *Music and Music Education History: A Chronology*. Lawrence, KS: Department of Art and Music Education and Music Therapy, 1993.

Holz, Emil A., and Roger E. Jacobi. *Teaching Band Instruments to Beginners*. Englewood Cliffs, NJ: Prentice-Hall, Inc., 1966.

Hood, Marguerite V. *Teaching Rhythm and Classroom Instruments*. Englewood Cliffs, NJ: Prentice-Hall, Inc., 1970.

Howe, Neil, and William Strauss. *Generations: The History of America's Future, 1584–2069*. New York: William Morrow and Company, Inc., 1991.

Knapp, Clyde Guy, and E. Patricia Hagman. *Teaching Methods for Physical Education: A Textbook for Secondary School Teachers*. New York: McGraw-Hill, 1953.

Knapp, Clyde Guy, and Patricia Hagman Leonhard. *Teaching Physical Education in Secondary Schools*. New York: McGraw-Hill, 1968.

Knowles, Patricia. *Annotated Directory for Dance Education*. Reston, VA: National Dance Association, 1991.

_____. *Dance Education in American Schools: Case Studies*. Urbana, IL: Council for Research in Music Education, 1991.

Kraus, Richard G. *Square Dances of Today and How to Teach and Call Them*. Illustrated by Carl Pfeufer, musical arrangements by Charles Leonhard. New York: A. S. Barnes and Company, 1950.

Krone, Max T., Irving Wolfe, Beatrice Perham Krone, and Margaret Fullerton. *Together We Sing*. 9 Vols. Chicago: Follett Publishing Company, 1951–58. Revised edition, 1959–64.

Langer, Susanne K. *Feeling and Form*. New York: Charles Scribner's Sons, 1953.

_____. *Philosophy in a New Key*. Cambridge, MA: Harvard University Press, 1942.

_____. *Problems of Art*. New York: Charles Scribner's Sons, 1957.

*Learning and Living Music*. Springfield, IL: Office of the Superintendent of Public Instruction, 1961.

Lehman, Paul R. *Tests and Measurements in Music*. Englewood Cliffs, NJ: Prentice-Hall, Inc., 1968.

Leonhard, Charles. *Recreation Through Music*. New York: A. S. Barnes, 1952.

_____. *A Song Approach to Music Reading*. New York: Silver Burdett Co., 1953.

_____. *The Status of Arts Education in American Public Schools*. Urbana, IL: Council for Research in Music Education, 1991.

_____. *The Status of Arts Education: Summary and Conclusions*. Urbana, IL: Council for Research in Music Education, 1991.

_____. *Words of Note: A Realistic Rationale for Teaching Music*. Reston, VA: Music Educators National Conference, 1985.

Leonhard, Charles, and Robert W. House. *Foundations and Principles of Music Education*. New York: McGraw-Hill Book Company, Inc., 1959.

_____. *Foundations and Principles of Music Education*. 2nd ed. New York: McGraw-Hill Book Company, 1972.

Leonhard, Charles, Beatrice Perham Krone, Irving Wolfe, and Margaret Fullerton. Discovering Music Together. 9 Vols. Chicago: Follett Publishing Company, 1966–68. Revised edition, 1970.

Leonhard, Charles. Beatrice Perham Krone, Irving Wolfe, Margaret Fullerton, and Robert B. Smith, *Discovering Music Together*. Teacher Education Edition. Chicago: Follett Educational Corporation, 1971.

Magee, Barbara. *Guidelines for the Development of Documents Addressing K-12 Dance Education Programs*. Urbana, IL: Dance Department, University of Illinois, 1991.

Mark, Michael L. *Contemporary Music Education*. 2nd ed. New York: Schirmer Books, 1986.

McConathy, Osbourne, Russell V. Morgan, James L. Mursell, Marshall Bartholomew, Mabel E. Bray, Edward Bailey Birge, and W. Otto Miessner. *World Music Horizons*, Book 5. Revised ed. New York: Silver Burdett Company, 1953.

McEachern, Edna. *A Survey and Evaluation of the Education of School Music Teachers in the United States*. Teachers College, Columbia University Contributions to Education, No. 701. New York: Teachers College, Columbia University, 1937.

Morris, Eleanor L., and John E. Bowes, eds. *Music Objectives*. Denver, CO: National Assessment of Educational Progress, Education Commission of the States, 1970

Mursell, James L. *Education for Musical Growth*. Boston: Ginn & Company, 1948.

_____. *Educational Psychology*. New York: W. W. Norton & Company, Inc., 1939.

_____. *Music Education Principles and Programs*. Morristown, NJ: Silver Burdett Company, 1956

_____. *Principles of Democratic Education.* New York: W. W. Norton & Company, Inc., 1955.

_____. *The Psychology of Music.* New York: W. W. Norton & Company, Inc., 1937.

_____. *The Psychology of Secondary-School Teaching.* New York: W. W. Norton & Company, 1939.

_____. *Successful Teaching: Its Psychological Principles.* New York: McGraw-Hill Book Company, Inc., 1946.

Mursell, James L., and Mabelle Glenn. *The Psychology of School Music Teaching.* New York: Silver Burdett Company, 1931.

*National School Music Competition-Festivals: 1941 Reports.* Chicago: National School Band, Orchestra and Vocal Associations, 1941.

Nordholm, Harriet. *Singing in the Elementary Schools.* Englewood Cliffs, NJ: Prentice-Hall, Inc., 1966.

Peters, G. David. *Musical Skills: A Computer-Based Assessment.* Urbana, IL: Council for Research in Music Education, 1991.

Pitts, Lilla Belle, Mabelle Glenn, Lorrain E. Watters, and Louis G. Wersen. Our Singing World, 9 vols. Boston: Ginn and Company, 1949–1957.

Reimer, Bennett. *A Philosophy of Music Education.* 2nd ed. Englewood Cliffs, NJ: Prentice Hall, 1989.

Shetler, Donald, ed. *In Memoriam Howard Hanson: The Future of Musical Education in America.* Rochester, NY: Eastman School of Music Press, 1984.

Stake, Robert, Liora Bresler, and Linda Mabry. *Custom and Cherishing: The Arts in Elementary Schools.* Urbana, IL: Council for Research in Music Education, 1991.

Tait, Malcolm, and Paul A. Haack. *Principles and Processes of Music Education: New Perspectives.* New York: Teachers College Press, 1984.

University of Illinois. *Graduate Catalog,* 1964–56. Urbana, IL: University of Illinois, 1964.

_____. *Transactions,* 1952–54. (Urbana, IL: University of Illinois, 1954).

_____. *Undergraduate Study,* 1952–53. Urbana, IL: University of Illinois, 1952.

_____. *Undergraduate Study,* 1954–55. Urbana, IL: University of Illinois, 1954.

_____. *Undergraduate Study,* 1964–65. Urbana, IL: University of Illinois, 1964.

University of Oklahoma. *University of Oklahoma Catalog,* 1932–33. Norman, OK: The University of Oklahoma, 1932.

_____. *University of Oklahoma Catalog,* 1936–37. Norman, OK: The University of Oklahoma, 1936.

*The WPA Guide to 1930s Oklahoma.* Lawrence, KS: The University Press of Kansas, 1986.

Wilson, George H., ed. *Current Issues in Music Education—A Symposium for College Teachers on Music Education.* Columbus, OH: The Ohio State University, 1963.

Wright, Lin, ed. *The Arizona State University K-6 Drama Theatre Curriculum Guide.* Urbana, IL: Council for Research in Music Education, 1991.

## Book Chapters

Abeles, Harold F., Charles R. Hoffer, and Robert H. Klotman. "Teacher Education and Future Directions." Chap. in *Foundations of Music Education*. New York: Schirmer Books, 1984.

"Audio-Visual Aids in Music Education." Chap. in *Music in American Education: Music Education Source Book Number Two*, ed. Hazel Nohavec Morgan. Chicago: Music Educators National Conference, 1955.

Boyd, Willard L. "Music: Basic Education." In *In Memoriam Howard Hanson: The Future of Musical Education in America*, ed. Donald Shetler, 49–59. Rochester, NY: Eastman School of Music Press, 1984.

Colwell, Richard J. "Dedication." In *Symposium in Music Education: A Festschrift for Charles Leonhard*. Urbana, IL: University of Illinois, 1982.

"Details on the 1981 Symposium in Music Education." In *Symposium in Music Education*, ed. Richard J. Colwell, v. Urbana, IL: University of Illinois, 1982.

Emerson, Ralph Waldo. "History." In *The Portable Emerson*, New edition, ed. Carl Bode and Malcolm Cowley, 115–137. New York: Viking Penguin, Inc., 1981.

Freeman, Robert. "On the Need for Bridging Music's Islands." In *In Memoriam Howard Hanson: The Future of Musical Education in America*, ed. Donald Shetler, 72–85. Rochester, NY: Eastman School of Music Press, 1984.

Gates, J. Terry. Foreword to *Music Education in the United States: Contemporary Issues*. Tuscaloosa, AL: The University of Alabama Press, 1988.

Getz, Russell P. "Music Education in Tomorrow's Schools: A Practical Approach." In *In Memoriam Howard Hanson: The Future of Musical Education in America*, ed. Donald Shetler, 21–31. Rochester, NY: Eastman School of Music Press, 1984.

Henry, Nelson B. "Editor's Preface." In *Basic Concepts in Music Education*, ed. Nelson B. Henry. Chicago: National Society for the Study of Education, 1958.

Hodkinson, Sidney. "The Phoenix Revisited: An Etude in Musicomythology." In *In Memoriam Howard Hanson: The Future of Musical Education in America*, ed. Donald Shetler, 32–48. Rochester, NY: Eastman School of Music Press, 1984.

Hodsoll, Frank S. M. "Arts Education and the Arts Endowment." In *In Memoriam Howard Hanson: The Future of Musical Education in America*, ed. Donald Shetler, 1–10. Rochester, NY: Eastman School of Music Press, 1984.

Hood, Marguerite V. "Music Educators Source Book No. 2." In *Music in American Education: Music Education Source Book Number Two*, ed. Hazel Nohavec Morgan, viii–ix. Chicago: Music Educators National Conference, 1955.

Lasch, Christopher. "The Degradation of Work and the Apotheosis of Art." In *In Memoriam Howard Hanson: The Future of Musical Education in America*, ed. Donald Shetler, 11–20. Rochester, NY: Eastman School of Music Press, 1984.

Leonhard, Charles. "Evaluation in Music Education." In *Basic Concepts in Music Education, the Fifty-Seventh Yearbook of the National Society for the Study of Education*, ed. Nelson B. Henry, 310–338. Chicago: National Society for the Study of Education, 1958.

_____. Foreword to *Administration in Music Education*, by Robert W. House. Englewood Cliffs, NJ: Prentice-Hall, Inc., 1973.

_____. Foreword to *Building Instructional Programs in Music Education*, by Robert G. Sidnell. Englewood Cliffs, NJ: Prentice-Hall, Inc., 1973.

_____. Foreword to *The Evaluation of Music Teaching and Learning*, by Richard J. Colwell. Englewood Cliffs, NJ: Prentice-Hall, Inc., 1970.

_____. Foreword to *Experimental Research in Music*, by Clifford K. Madsen and Charles H. Madsen, Jr. Englewood Cliffs, NJ: Prentice-Hall, Inc., 1970.

_____. Foreword to *A Philosophy of Music Education*, by Bennett Reimer. Englewood Cliffs, NJ: Prentice-Hall, Inc., 1970.

_____. Foreword to *The Psychology of Music Teaching*, by Edwin E. Gordon. Englewood Cliffs, NJ: Prentice-Hall, Inc., 1971.

_____. "The Future of Musical Education in America: A Pragmatist's View." In *In Memoriam Howard Hanson: The Future of Musical Education in America*, ed. Donald J. Shetler, 60–71. Rochester, NY: Eastman School of Music Press, 1984.

_____. "The Human Values of Music Education." In *Music Education in the United States: Contemporary Issues*, ed. J. Terry Gates, 185–192. Tuscaloosa, AL: The University of Alabama Press, 1988.

_____. "Learning Theory and Music Teaching." In *Comprehensive Musicianship: The Foundation for College Education in Music*, 49–58. Washington, DC: Music Educators National Conference, 1965. [See also, *Current Issues in Music Education* 1 (1963) and *Bulletin of the Council for Research in Music Education* 1 (1963).]

_____. "Methods Courses in Music Teacher Education." In *Music Education in the United States: Contemporary Issues*, ed. J. Terry Gates, 193–201. Tuscaloosa, AL: The University of Alabama Press, 1988.

_____. "Music Teacher Education in the United States." In *Symposium in Music Education*, ed. Richard J. Colwell, 233–247. Urban, IL: University of Illinois, 1982.

_____. "The Philosophy of Music Education—Present and Future." In *Comprehensive Musicianship: The Foundation for College Education in Music*, 42–49. Washington, DC: Music Educators National Conference, 1965.

_____. "Reading Music." In *American Music Horizons*, Music Horizons Series, ed. Osbourne McConathy, Russell V. Morgan, James L. Mursell, Marshall Bartholomew, Mabel E. Bray, Edward Bailey Birge, and W. Otto Miessner, 267–276. New York: Silver Burdett Company, 1951. See also, *World Music Horizons*, New Music Horizons Series, ed. Osbourne McConathy, Russell V. Morgan, James L. Mursell, Marshall Bartholomew, Mabel E. Bray, Edward Bailey Birge, and W. Otto Miessner, 251– 259. New York: Silver Burdett Company, 1951.

McMurray, Foster. "Pragmatism in Music Education." In *Basic Concepts in Music Education*, ed. Nelson B. Henry, 30–61. Chicago: National Society for the Study of Education , 1958.

Murphy, Howard A. "The Duality of Music." In *Music in American Education: Music Education Source Book Number Two*, ed. Hazel Nohavec Morgan, 17. Chicago: Music Educators National Conference, 1955.

Mursell, James L. "Growth Processes in Music Education." In *Basic Concepts in Music Education*, ed. Nelson B. Henry, 140–162. Chicago: National Society for the Study of Education, 1958.

"Recommendations of Group II: Musical Analysis and Aural Skills." In *Comprehensive Musicianship: The Foundation for College Education in Music*, 14–17. Washington, DC: Music Educators National Conference, 1965.

## Periodicals, Newspapers, Dictionaries, and Books of Proceedings

"Banquet for Teachers Has Big Attendance." *The Duncan* [Oklahoma] *Banner*, 21 November 1937, 7.

Bennett, Barbara L. "The Charles Leonhard Oral History Memoirs." *Southeastern Journal of Music Education* 4 (1992): 84–100.

_____. "The Leonhard Connection." *Bulletin of the Council for Research in Music Education* 100 (Fall 1991): 3–20.

*Biographical Dictionary of American Educators*, 1978 ed. S.v., "Counts, George Sylvester," by Ralph E. Ackerman; and "Rugg, Harold Ordway," by Murray R. Nelson

Boardman, Eunice L., "Society for Music Teacher Education: The Formative Years." *Journal of Music Teacher Education* 1 (Spring 1992): 2–4.

"Choir Guild Chooses Two." *The Duncan* [Oklahoma] *Banner*, 9 November 1937, 6.

"Choir Guild to Be Active in Second Year." *The Duncan* [Oklahoma] *Banner*, 19 October 1937, 8.

Crockett, Frank. "Georgia Scene." *Georgia Music News* 26 (February 1966): 24.

Davidson, James W., and Charles Leonhard. "The Illinois Curriculum Program and Music Education," *Music Educators Journal* 39 (June-July 1953): 40–42.

"Dr. Goodwin Watson, Taught at Columbia." *New York Times*, 5 January 1977, B 18.

Edwards, June. "Indoctrination into Freedom: John Childs Speaks for Today." *Contemporary Education* 58 (Fall 1986): 18–21.

Eisenstadt, Jeanne Watson. "Remembering Goodwin Watson." *Journal of Social Issues* 42 (1986): 49–52.

Eisner, Elliot W. "Two Portraits of Arts Education: Homegrown in the Midwest." *Educational Researcher* 22 (January–February 1993): 32–34.

*Encyclopedia of Education*, 1971. S.v., "Music Education: 1. Elementary Schools," by O. M Hartsell; "Music Education: 2. Secondary Schools," by Richard J. Colwell; "Music Education: 3. Colleges," by Charles Leonhard and Gary R. Sudano; "Music Education: 4. Jazz," by M. E. Hall; "Music Education: 5. Education of American Composers," by Grant Beglarian; "Music Education: 6. Training of Teachers," by Robert H. Klotman; "Music Education: 7. Supervision in the Schools," by Charles L. Gary; Music Education: 8. Evaluation," by Paul R. Lehman; and "Music Education: 9. Changing Goals," by Charles B. Fowler.

"Graduate Study in Music Education." *Journal of Research in Music Education* 2 (Fall 1954): 157–179.

This was a report of a sub-committee of the MENC Committee on Music in Higher Education which served from 1951 to 1954. Theodore F. Normann chaired the Sub-Committee on Graduate

Study in Music Education. Oleta A. Benn, Allen P. Britton, William R. Fisher, E. Thayer Gaston, Wiley L. Housewright, C. B. Hunt, William E. Knuth, Charles Leonhard, Thurber H. Madison, Hazel Nohavec Morgan, Howard Murphy, Anne E. Pierce, Ralph E. Rush, David Stone, Lloyd F. Sunderman, Everett Timm, and Jack Watson served on it.

Izdebski, Christy, and Michael L. Mark. "Vanett Lawler: International Music Education Administrator." *The Bulletin of Historical Research in Music Education* 8 (January 1987): 1–32.

"Junior High's Operetta to Be Ready Friday." *The Duncan* [Oklahoma] *Banner*, 1 December 1937, 11.

Kersey, Ethel M. *Women Philosophers: A Bio-Critical Source Book.* New York: Greenwood Press, 1989. S.v. "Langer, Susanne Katherina Knauth."

Leonhard, Charles. "Aesthetic Education in a World of Numbers." In *Fourth Annual Leadership Conference in Music Education: Summary Report,* 29–34. Springfield, IL: Office of the Superintendent of Public Instruction, State of Illinois, 1971. See also, *The Canadian Music Educator* 12 (Summer 1971): 5–7; and *The British Columbia Music Educator* 15 (October 1971): 34–37.

_____. "Aesthetic Literacy in Music." *Design for Arts in Education* 92 (September–October 1991): 27–29.

_____. "The Challenge." *Bulletin of the Council for Research in Music Education* 117 (Summer 1993): 1–8.

_____. "A Challenge to Music Educators: A Twelve-Year Coordinated Music Program." *Oklahoma School Music News* 12 (December 1961): 3–7.

_____. "A Classroom Teacher and Music Reading." *The Resourceful Teacher* 6 (1952): 12–19.

_____. "Disc Jockey in the Classroom." *NEA Journal* 39 (November 1950): 588–589.

_____. "An Easier Way to Read Music." *Music Journal* 11 (March 1953): 28, and 49–55.

_____. "Expand Your Classroom." *Music Educators Journal* 68 (November 1981): 54, and 61–62.

_____. Foreword. *Bulletin of the Council for Research in Music Education* 81 (Winter 1985): 1–3.

_____. "The Great Masquerade: Means Become Ends." *Missouri School Music Magazine* 35 (Spring 1981): 30–31, and 40.

_____. "Has Jazz Education Fulfilled Its Promise?" *Jazz Educators Journal* 16 (December–January 1984): 12–13, and 98.

_____. "Human Potential and the Aesthetic Experience." *Music Educators Journal* 54 (April 1968): 39–41, and 109–111.

_____. "Humanizing Music in a Mechanized Society." *Music Educators Journal* 68 (May 1982): 23–24.

_____. "Lifelong Learning in Music: A Challenge to Music Educators." In *Loyola Music Symposium IV: Music in Community Education*, ed. David Swanzy and William S. English, 33–39. New Orleans, LA: Loyola University, 1981.

_____. "Means and Ends in Music Education." *Florida Music Director* 35 (December 1981): 10–11.

_____. "Music." *Review of Educational Research* 25 (April 1955): 166–175.

_____. "Music Education." *Review of Educational Research* 28 (April 1958): 159–168.

_____. "Music Education—Aesthetic Education." *Education* 74 (September 1953): 23–26.

_____. "Music Education: A Socially Significant Enterprise." *Florida Music Director* 35 (March 1982): 6–7.

_____. "The National Arts Education Research Center." *Bulletin of the Council for Research in Music Education* 105 (Summer 1990): 1–21.

_____. "A New Approach to Music Theory." *MTNA Proceedings* (1949): 207–214.

_____. "Newer Concepts in Learning Theory as They Apply to Music Education." *Bulletin of the Council for Research in Music Education Bulletin* 1 (June 1963): 24–31. See also, "Newer Concepts in Learning Theory as They Apply to Music Education." In *Current Issues in Music Education: A Symposium for College Teachers of Music Education*, ed. George H. Wilson, 1–9. Columbus, OH: The Ohio State University, 1963; and "Learning Theory and Music Teaching." In *Comprehensive Musicianship: The Foundation for College Education in Music*, 42–49. Washington, DC: Music Educators National Conference, 1965.

Leonhard, Charles, Allen P. Britton, and Paul R. Lehman, "Developing Researchers in Music Education." In *A Conference on Research in Music Education*, ed. Henry L. Cady, 34–38. Columbus, OH: The Ohio State University, 1967.

_____. "The Next Ten Years." *Music Educators Journal* 55 (September 1968): 48–50.

_____. "The Next Ten Years in Music Education." *Bulletin of the Council for Research in Music Education* 7 (Spring 1966): 13–23.

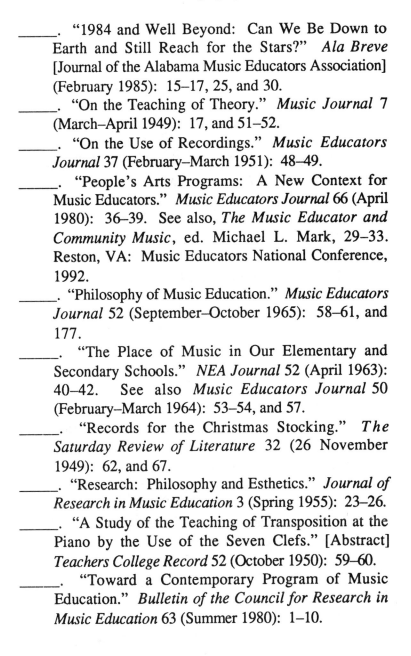

_____. "1984 and Well Beyond: Can We Be Down to Earth and Still Reach for the Stars?" *Ala Breve* [Journal of the Alabama Music Educators Association] (February 1985): 15–17, 25, and 30.

_____. "On the Teaching of Theory." *Music Journal* 7 (March–April 1949): 17, and 51–52.

_____. "On the Use of Recordings." *Music Educators Journal* 37 (February–March 1951): 48–49.

_____. "People's Arts Programs: A New Context for Music Educators." *Music Educators Journal* 66 (April 1980): 36–39. See also, *The Music Educator and Community Music*, ed. Michael L. Mark, 29–33. Reston, VA: Music Educators National Conference, 1992.

_____. "Philosophy of Music Education." *Music Educators Journal* 52 (September–October 1965): 58–61, and 177.

_____. "The Place of Music in Our Elementary and Secondary Schools." *NEA Journal* 52 (April 1963): 40–42. See also *Music Educators Journal* 50 (February–March 1964): 53–54, and 57.

_____. "Records for the Christmas Stocking." *The Saturday Review of Literature* 32 (26 November 1949): 62, and 67.

_____. "Research: Philosophy and Esthetics." *Journal of Research in Music Education* 3 (Spring 1955): 23–26.

_____. "A Study of the Teaching of Transposition at the Piano by the Use of the Seven Clefs." [Abstract] *Teachers College Record* 52 (October 1950): 59–60.

_____. "Toward a Contemporary Program of Music Education." *Bulletin of the Council for Research in Music Education* 63 (Summer 1980): 1–10.

_____. "Toward Reform in Music Teacher Education." *Bulletin of the Council for Research in Music Education* 81 (Winter 1985): 10–17.

_____. "Trends in the Future of Music Education." *The Nebraska Music Educator* 33 (April 1975): 2, and 11. See also, *The Illinois Music Educator* 36 (Summer 1976): 8.

_____. "Was the Yale Seminar Worthwhile?" *Bulletin of the Council for Research in Music Education* 60 (Fall 1979): 61–64.

_____. "Where's the Beef?" *The Bulletin of Historical Research in Music Education* 3 (July 1985): 58–60.

Leonhard, Charles, and Richard J. Colwell. "Research in Music Education." *Bulletin of the Council for Research in Music Education* 49 (Winter 1976): 1–30. See also, *Arts and Aesthetics: An Agenda for the Future*, ed. Stanley S. Madeja, 81–108. St. Louis, MO: CEMREL, Inc., 1977.

"Leonhard to Give Recital," *The Duncan* [Oklahoma] *Banner*, 6 October 1937.

Madeja, Stanley S. "The Aesthetics of Education: The CEMREL Aesthetic Education Program." *Bulletin of the Council for Research in Music Education* 43 (Summer 1975): 1–18.

Mead, Rita H. "The Amazing Mr. Cowell." *American Music* 1 (Winter 1983): 63–89.

"'Moon Maiden' Matinee Today," *The Duncan* [Oklahoma] *Banner*, 2 December 1937, 6.

"Music Education." *Teachers College Record* 53 (October 1951): 54.

*Music Educators Journal* 59 (May 1973): 47.

"National School Music Competition Festivals," *Oklahoma Agricultural and Mechanical College Bulletin*, March 1941, 36–37, 41–44, and 75.

*The New Grove Dictionary of American Music*, 1986 ed. S.v. "Bauer, Harold," by H. C. Colles and Ronald Kinloch Anderson; "Britton, Allen P.," by Paula Morgan; "Cowell, Henry (Dixon)," by Bruce Saylor, William Lichtenwanger, and Elizabeth A. Wright; "Dykema, Peter W.," by George N. Heller; "Herford, Julius"; "Kolodin, Irving," by Patrick J. Smith; "Langer, Susanne K.," by F. E. Sparshott and Paula Morgan; "Mursell, James L.," by George N. Heller; "Pitts, Lilla Belle," by George N. Heller; "Reimer, Bennett," by George N. Heller; "Seashore, Carl E.," by Ramona H. Matthews; and "Sherwood, William H.," by Robert Groves.

"Oklahoma Interscholastic Music Contest," *Oklahoma Agricultural and Mechanical College Bulletin*, December 1938, 46, and 51–52.

"Oklahoma Interscholastic Music Contest," *Oklahoma Agricultural and Mechanical College Bulletin*, December 1939, 40–41, and 44–45.

Rosenblatt, Bernard S., and Rene Michel-Trapaga. "Through the Teacher to the Child: Aesthetic Education for Teachers," *Bulletin of the Council for Research in Music Education* 43 (Summer 1975): 46–47.

"School Parade Today Moved to Later Date." *The Duncan* [Oklahoma] *Banner*, 10 November 1937, 1.

Simutis, Leonard J. "James L. Mursell: An Annotated Bibliography." *Journal of Research in Music Education* 16 (Fall 1968): 254–266.

Smith, Ralph A., ed. *Cultural Literacy and Arts Education*. Special issue of the *Journal of Aesthetic Education* 24 (Spring 1990).

"Stillwater, Bristow Are High in Instrumental Work." *Daily O'Collegian* [Oklahoma A & M Student newspaper], 8 May 1931, 1.

"Subjects High School Faculty Will Teach This Year Listed." *The Duncan* [Oklahoma] *Banner*, 2 September 1937, 1.

*Teachers College Record* 53 (October 1951).

"Tenors Scarce at Duncan High; All Boys Want to Sing Bass." *The Duncan* [Oklahoma] *Banner*, 5 October 1937.

"Two New Members Are Welcomed into Duncan Music Club." *The Duncan* [Oklahoma] *Banner*, 10 October 1937, 7.

Van Til, William. "John L. Childs: An Appreciation." *Contemporary Education* 58 (Fall 1986): 21.

*Who's Who in America*, 1990–91. S.v. "Boardman, Eunice"; and "Colwell, Richard James."

Wolfe, Irving W. "Rural School Music Missionary," *Music Educators Journal* 46 (April–May 1960): 26–28.

## Book Reviews

"Book Reviews." *Journal of the American Medical Association* 149 (2 August 1952): 1357.

Crews, E. Katherine. Review of *Foundations and Principles of Music Education*, 2nd ed., by Charles Leonhard and Robert W. House. In *Music Educators Journal* 59 (March 1973): 82–86.

Hanshumaker, James R. Review of *Building Instructional Programs in Music Education*, by Robert G. Sidnell. In *Journal of Research in Music Education* 22 (Winter 1974): 330–331.

Kyme, George. Review of *The Evaluation of Music Teaching and Learning*, by Richard J. Colwell. In *Journal of Research in Music Education* 19 (Fall 1971): 380–381.

Lehman, Paul R. Review of *Foundations and Principles of Music Education*, 2nd ed., by Charles Leonhard and Robert W. House. In *Journal of Research in Music Education* 21 (Summer 1973): 190–191.

Leonhard, Charles. Review of *The Enjoyment of Music: An Introduction to Perceptive Listening*, by Joseph Machlis. In *Journal of Research in Music Education* 3 (Fall 1955): 149.

_____. Review of *An Introduction to Music and Art in the Western World*, by Milo Wold and Edmund Cykler. In *Journal of Research in Music Education* 7 (Spring 1959): 151–152.

_____. Review of *Jean Sibelius*, by Jils-Eric Ringbom. In *Journal of Research in Music Education* 3 (Spring 1955): 66–67.

_____. Review of *Music and Recordings 1955*, by Frederic V. Grunfield and Quaintance Eaton. In *Journal of Research in Music Education* 4 (Spring 1956): 59–60.

_____. Review of *Music Education in Action*, by Russell Van Dyke Morgan and Hazel Nohavec Morgan. In *Journal of Research in Music Education* 2 (Fall 1954): 188–189.

_____. Review of *Music Education: Principles and Programs*, by James L. Mursell. In *Journal of Research in Music Education* 5 (Spring 1957): 46–47.

_____. Review of *An Objective Psychology of Music*, by Robert W. Lundin. In *Journal of Research in Music Education* 1 (Fall 1953): 141–143.

_____. Review of *Writing About Music: A Style Book for Reports and Theses*, by Demar Irvine. In *Journal of Research in Music Education* 5 (Spring 1957): 59.

*Library Journal*, 15 May 1952, 899.

Normann, Theodore F. Review of *Foundations and Principles of Music Education*, by Charles Leonhard and Robert W. House. In *Journal of Research in Music Education* 8 (Spring 1960): 51–53.

_____. Review of *Foundations and Principles of Music Education*, by Charles Leonhard and Robert W. House. In *Music Educators Journal* 46 (February–March 1960): 110.

Nye, Robert E. Review of *A Song Approach to Music Reading*, by Charles Leonhard. In *Journal of Research in Music Education* 1 (Fall 1953): 150–151.

"Peabody Bimonthly Booknotes." *Peabody Journal of Education* 30 (September 1952): 120.

Review of *Foundations and Principles of Music Education*, by Charles Leonhard and Robert W. House. *The Instrumentalist* 14 (February 1960): 6.

Review of *Foundations and Principles of Music Education*, 2nd ed., by Charles Leonhard and Robert W. House. In *The American Music Teacher* 22 (November–December 1972): 43.

Schwadron, Abraham A. Review of *A Philosophy of Music Education*, by Bennett Reimer. In *Journal of Research in Music Education* 19 (Summer 1971): 253–255.

## Theses and Dissertations

NB: Dissertations listed here are those cited in the text. The Appendix contains the entire list of dissertations for which Leonhard was the advisor, most of which are not cited in the text.

Birkner, Thomas F. "An Analysis and Classification of Conductor Vocal Communication in the Rehearsals of Selected Jazz Ensembles." Ed.D. diss., University of Illinois, 1992.

Blanchard, Gerald L. "Lilla Belle Pitts: Her Life and Contribution to Music Education." Ed.D. diss., Brigham Young University, 1966.

Davidson, James W. "Construction and Appraisal of Procedures and Materials for Developing Consensus Regarding Music Education Programs." Ed. D. diss., University of Illinois, 1954.

Delaney, Carole. "The Contribution of Marion Flagg to Music and Education." D.M.A. diss., The University of Texas, 1974.

Eisenkramer, Henry E. "Peter William Dykema: His Life and Contribution to Music Education." Ed.D. diss., Teachers College, Columbia University, 1963.

Foust, Diane. "Musical Theatre Education: A Case Study." Ed.D. diss., University of Illinois, 1992.

Fry, Raymond J. "Development and Trial of a Computer Based Interactive Videodisc Program in a Course in Fundamentals of Conducting." Ed.D. diss., University of Illinois, 1991.

Goss, Donald R. "Irving W. Wolfe: His Life and Contributions to Music Education." Ph.D. diss., George Peabody College for Teachers, 1972.

Harrison, Albert D. "A History of the University of Illinois School of Music, 1940–1970." Ed.D. diss., University of Illinois, 1986.

Johnston William L. "An Appraisal of Music Programs in the Public Schools of Illinois Excluding Chicago." Ed.D. diss., The University of Illinois, 1966.

Kritzmire, Judith A. "The Pedagogy of Charles Leonhard: A Documentary Case Study." Ed.D. diss., The University of Illinois, 1987.

Leonhard, Charles. "A Study of the Teaching of Transposition at the Piano by the Use of the Seven Clefs." Ed.D. diss., Teachers College, Columbia University, 1949.

Metz, Donald E. "A Critical Analysis of the Thought of James L. Mursell in Music Education." Ph.D. diss., Case Western Reserve University, 1968.

O'Keefe, Vincent C. "James Lockhart Mursell, His Life and Contributions to Music Education." Ed.D. diss., Teachers College, Columbia University, 1970.

Olsen, Richard Norman. "Howard A. Murphy, Theorist and Teacher: His Influence on the Teaching of Basic Music Theory in American Colleges and Universities from 1940 to 1973." Ed.D. diss., University of Illinois, 1973.

Prince, Joe N. "An Evaluation of Graduate Music Education Programs at the University of Illinois." Ed.D. diss., University of Illinois, 1968.

Reed, Larry Woods. "The History of the Department of Music and Music Education Teachers College, Columbia University—The Early Years: 1887–1939." Ed.D. diss., Teachers College, Columbia University, 1982.

Sheckler, Lewis R. "Charles Alexander Fullerton: His Life and Contribution to Music Education." Ed.D. diss., University of Illinois, 1965.

Simutis, Leonard J. "James L. Mursell as Music Educator." Ph.D. diss., University of Ottawa, 1961.


## Letters


Britton, Allen P., Ann Arbor, MI, to George N. Heller, Lawrence, KS, 18 January 1989. Original in possession of the author.

Britton, Allen P., Ann Arbor, MI, to George N. Heller, Lawrence, KS, 18 February 1989. Original in possession of the author.

Colwell, Richard J., Greeley, CO, to George N. Heller, Lawrence, KS, 11 February 1990. Original in possession of the author.

Dinsmore, Donna, Spartanburg, SC, to Charles Leonhard, Urbana, IL, 24 November 1993. Photocopy in possession of the author.

Hilton, Lewis B., St. Louis, MO, to George N. Heller, Lawrence, KS, 3 February 1990. Original in possession of the author.

House, Robert W., Commerce, TX, to George N. Heller, Lawrence, KS, 23 March 1990. Original in possession of the author.

Housewright, Wiley L., Tallahassee, FL, to George N. Heller, Lawrence, KS, 27 February 1990. Original in possession of the author.

John, Robert W., Athens, GA, to George N. Heller, Lawrence, KS, 27 February 1990. Original in possession of the author.

Krone, Beatrice Perham. Idyllwild, CA, to George N. Heller, Lawrence, KS, 8 July 1990. Original in possession of the author.

Leonhard, Charles, Urbana, IL, to George L. Duerksen, Lawrence, KS, 20 September 1988. Photocopy in possession of the author.

Leonhard, Charles, Urbana, IL, to George N. Heller, Lawrence, KS, 25 February 1982. Original in possession of the author.

Leonhard, Charles, Urbana, IL, to George N. Heller, Lawrence, KS, 14 October 1982. Original in possession of the author.

Leonhard, Charles, Urbana, IL, to George N. Heller, Lawrence, KS, 25 April 1983. Original in possession of the author.

Leonhard, Charles, Urbana, IL, to George N. Heller, Lawrence, KS, 24 October 1983. Original in possession of the author.

Leonhard, Charles, Urbana, IL, to George N. Heller, Lawrence, KS, 4 January 1984. Original in possession of the author.

Leonhard, Charles, Urbana, IL, to George N. Heller, Lawrence, KS, 5 April 1984. Original in possession of the author.

Leonhard, Charles, Urbana, IL, to George N. Heller, Lawrence, KS, 11 September 1984. Original in possession of the author.

Leonhard, Charles, Urbana, IL, to George N. Heller, Lawrence, KS, 22 October 1984. Original in possession of the author.

Leonhard, Charles, Urbana, IL, to George N. Heller, Lawrence, KS, 5 August 1985. Original in possession of the author.

Leonhard, Charles, Urbana, IL, to George N. Heller, Lawrence, KS, 11 May 1988. Original in possession of the author.

Leonhard, Charles, Urbana, IL, to George N. Heller, Lawrence, KS, 20 September 1988. Original in possession of the author.

Leonhard, Charles, Urbana, IL, to George N. Heller, Lawrence, KS, n.d. [Fall 1988]. Original in possession of the author.

Leonhard, Charles, Urbana, IL, to George N. Heller, Lawrence, KS, n.d. [1 January 1989]. Original in possession of the author.

Leonhard, Charles, Urbana, IL, to George N. Heller, Lawrence, KS, 8 June 1989. Original in possession of the author.

Leonhard, Charles, Urbana, IL, to George N. Heller, Lawrence, KS, 17 July 1989. Original in possession of the author.

Leonhard, Charles, Urbana, IL, to George N. Heller, Lawrence, KS, 18 September 1989. Original in possession of the author.

Leonhard, Charles, Urbana, IL, to George N. Heller, Lawrence, KS, 23 January 1990. Original in possession of the author.

Leonhard, Charles, Urbana, IL, to George N. Heller, Lawrence, KS, 10 February 1993. Original in possession of the author.

Leonhard, Charles, Urbana, IL, to George N. Heller, Lawrence, KS, 25 March 1993. Original in possession of the author.

Leonhard, Charles, Urbana, IL, to George N. Heller, Lawrence, KS, 17 May 1993. Original in possession of the author.

Leonhard, Charles, Urbana, IL, to George N. Heller, Lawrence, KS, 1 June 1993. Original in possession of the author.

Leonhard, Charles, Urbana, IL, to George N. Heller, Lawrence, KS, 9 June 1993. Original in possession of the author.

Leonhard, Charles, Urbana, IL, to George N. Heller, Lawrence, KS, 7 July 1993. Original in possession of the author.

Leonhard, Charles, Urbana, IL, to George N. Heller, Lawrence, KS, 4 August 1993. Original in possession of the author.

Leonhard, Charles, Urbana, IL, to George N. Heller, Lawrence, KS, 25 August 1993. Original in possession of the author.

Leonhard, Charles, Urbana, IL, to George N. Heller, Lawrence, KS, 29 September 1993. Original in possession of the author.

Leonhard, Charles, Urbana, IL, to George N. Heller, Lawrence, KS, 6 October 1993. Original in possession of the author.

Leonhard, Charles, Urbana, IL, to George N. Heller, Lawrence, KS, 20 October 1993. Original in possession of the author.

Leonhard, Charles, Urbana, IL, to George N. Heller, Lawrence, KS, 1 November 1993. Original in possession of the author.

Leonhard, Charles, Urbana, IL, to George N. Heller and John W. Grashel, Lawrence, KS, 5 April 1984. Original in possession of the author.

Leonhard, Charles, Urbana, IL, to Professors Clifford and Charles Madsen, Tallahassee, FL, 21 June 1968. Photocopy in possession of the author

Leonhard, Charles, Urbana, IL, to Bruce D. Wilson, College Park, MD 26 January 1989. Photocopy in possession of the author.

Madsen, Clifford K., Tallahassee, FL, to George N. Heller, Lawrence, KS, 24 October 1990. Original in possession of the author.

Madsen, Clifford K., and Charles H. Madsen, Tallahassee, FL, to Charles Leonhard, Urbana, IL, 22 July 1968. Photocopy in possession of the author

McAdams, Charles A., Warrensburg, MO, to George N. Heller, Lawrence, KS, 3 November 1993. Original in possession of the author

McRae, Jack A., Chickasha, OK, to George N. Heller, Lawrence, KS, 5 February 1990. Original in possession of the author.

Platt, Melvin, Norman, OK, to George N. Heller, Lawrence, KS, 19 July 1989. Original in possession of the author.

President of Teachers College, New York, NY, to Charles Leonhard, New York, NY, 8 February 1950. Photocopy in possession of the author.

President of Teachers College, New York, NY, to Charles Leonhard, New York, NY, 10 February 1950. Photocopy in possession of the author.

Worrel, J. William, Cincinnati, OH, to George N. Heller, Lawrence, KS, 9 March 1990. Original in possession of the author.

## Personal Interviews

Boardman, Eunice L. Interview by author, 14 October 1990, Champaign, IL. Tape recording and transcript in possession of the author.

Leonhard, Charles. Interview by author, 13 October 1990, Urbana, IL. Tape recording and transcript in possession of the author.

Melton, Marie (Penny) Cummins (Mrs. Truman). Interview by author, 12 February 1990, Anadarko, OK. Tape recording and transcript in possession of the author.

Walker, Lauraleen Farnham Moore (Mrs. Charles). Interview by author, 10 February 1990, Duncan, OK. Tape recording and transcript in possession of the author.

Wood, Dion C., and LaVerne Moore Smith. Interview by author, 11 February 1990, Duncan, OK. Tape recording and transcript in possession of the author.

## Miscellaneous

*The Argus* [Oklahoma College for Women Yearbook] (1929). University Archive, University of Science and the Arts, Chickasha, OK.

*The Arts and Technology in a Community-Based School: A Design for Excellence in Education.* A proposal to the New American Schools Development Corporation from the University of Illinois at Urbana-Champaign and the Illinois Alliance for Arts Education, with the cooperation of the Kennedy Center for the Performing Arts (Urbana, IL College of Fine and Applied Arts, University of Illinois, n. d. [1993]).

Bennett, Barbara L. "Guide to the Charles Leonhard Special Collection in Music Education." TMs [photocopy], Charles Leonhard Special Collection in Music Education, School of Music, Baylor University, Waco, TX.

*Demon Round-Up* [Duncan, Oklahoma, High School Yearbook] (1941).

"Early History of Anadarko." Loose leaf material on file in the Anadarko Philomathic Museum, Anadarko, OK.

"The Future of Arts Education: Arts Teacher Education." Program, National Arts Education Research Center and The College of Fine and Applied Arts, The University of Illinois at Urbana, Champaign, 1992.

Heller, George N. Handwritten notes taken at Charles Leonhard's speech to the Kansas Council of Music Teacher Education Programs at Rock Springs Ranch, near Junction City, KS, 16 September 1982. Handwritten on conference program. Original in possession of the author.

_____. Handwritten notes taken at Charles Leonhard's speech to the Music Educators National Conference, 12 February 1982, San Antonio Texas. Original in possession of the author.

Kirk, Colleen J. Cassette tape response, Tallahassee, FL, 24 March 1990, Tape and transcript in possession of the author.

Leonhard, Charles. "Can We Continue to Teach the Lyre?" Paper presented at the Graduate Music Education Forum, University of Cincinnati, Cincinnati, OH, 29 April 1990.

_____. Contract for Assistant Professor of Music Education, Teachers College, Columbia University, 10 February 1950. Photocopy in possession of the author.

_____. Diploma for Bachelor of Fine arts in Public School Music, University of Oklahoma, 1937. Photocopy in possession of the author.

_____. Diploma for Doctor of Education, Teachers College, Columbia University, 1949. Photocopy in possession of the author.

_____. Discharge papers, U. S. Army, 16 May 1946. Photocopy in possession of the author.

_____. Letter of promotion to Assistant Professor, Teachers College, Columbia University, 8 February 1950. Photocopy in possession of the author.

_____. Memorandum to Persons Attending the Session of the Council on Music Teacher Education at San Antonio, 2 August 1982. Photocopy in possession of the author.

_____. Memorandum to Persons Attending the San Antonio Meeting of the Council on Music Teacher Education, n. d. [after 9 October 1982]. Photocopy in possession of the author.

_____. "Music and Musical Education: On the Way to the Promised Land." Paper presented at Baylor University, 10 March 1990.

_____. "Music Education—Aesthetic Education in the Real World of the School." Cassette recording, read by Leonhard, Music Educators National Conference, n.d. [1985].

_____. "The Past, The Present, and Their Portent for the Future." Paper presented at the Symposium in Honor of the Sesquicentennial of Public School Music (1838–1938), The University of Maryland, College Park, Maryland, 27 August, 1988.

_____. "A Proposal for Research in Arts Education." Remarks made at the Symposium on the Arts in American Schools: Setting a Research Agency for the 1990s," Annapolis, MD, 18 May, 1992. TMs (photocopy) in possession of the author.

_____. "The Status of Arts Education in American Public Schools." Pre-conference commissioned paper, The Arts in American Schools: Setting a Research Agenda for the 1990s, Annapolis, MD, 17–20 May 1992.

_____. Transcript of work at the Teachers College, Columbia University, summer session 1938 through spring session, 1948-49. Photocopy in possession of the author.

_____. Transcript of work at the University of Oklahoma, issued to the student 14 September 1937. Photocopy in possession of the author.

"National Arts Education Research Center—UIUC." Brochure, National Arts Education Research Center, Urbana, IL, n. d. [1993].

"Oklahoma Teacher's Register of Attendance and Scholarship, Grade 10 Through 12, 1932–1936." Principal's office, Anadarko High School, Anadarko, OK.

Peters, G. David. "National Arts Education Research Center: An Overview and Futureview." Paper presented at the Symposium on Educational Leadership in the Arts: Music as Art, Science and Entertainment, University of North Carolina at Chapel Hill, 25 September 1993.

*Sooner* [University of Oklahoma Yearbook] (1934, 1937). University Archive, Western History Collection, University of Oklahoma, Norman, OK.

# INDEX

# ABOUT THE AUTHOR

GEORGE N. HELLER is Professor of Music Education at The University of Kansas, where he has been on the faculty since 1973. Professor Heller has earned the bachelor's, master's, and doctoral degrees from The University of Michigan. He taught in public schools in Petersburg, Haslett, and Farmington, Michigan, and served in U. S. Army Bands at Ft. Sheridan, Illinois, and Heidelberg, Germany. Dr. Heller's special interests include secondary general music methods, ethnic music, and the history of music education and music therapy. He has edited *The Bulletin of Historical Research in Music Education* since 1980, and was the Music Education area advisor for *The New Grove Dictionary of American Music* (1986). Professor Heller is currently Southwestern Division chair of the Society for Music Teacher Education, and he serves on the Executive Committee of the Society for Research in Music Education. He is also on the editorial committees of *The Bulletin of the Council for Research in Music Education* and *The Quarterly Journal for Music Teaching and Learning.*